hm
STUDY SKILLS
PROGRAM
LEVEL III

Developed by The Study Skills Group

Author: Elaine M. Fitzpatrick, Ed.D.

Senior Editor: David Marshak
                   Bureau of Study Counsel
                   Harvard University

Editors: Kiyo Morimoto, *Director*
                   Bureau of Study Counsel
                   Harvard University

                   Jerome Pieh, *Headmaster*
                   Milton Academy

                   James J. McGuinn

American Council on Education
Washington, D.C. 20036

The National Association of Secondary School Principals
Reston, Virginia 22091

ISBN 0-88210-139-0

TABLE OF CONTENTS

INTRODUCTION

Study skills are *learning skills*. One term is old, the other relatively new, but both have similar meanings. Study skills include a wide array of procedures which promote effective learning and good academic performance. These skills for learning also help students make good use of their time and resources.

STUDY SKILLS: WHAT ARE THEY?

Study skills are primarily information-processing procedures which facilitate the learning, retention, and application of knowledge and skill. Although some students may learn these procedures spontaneously or incidentally as a result of other instruction, most students learn study skills effectively only through direct, focused instruction.

Study skills, then, are learned abilities for acquiring and applying knowledge and skill. Learning study skills involves *learning how to learn*.

TRANSITION FROM HIGH SCHOOL TO COLLEGE

When students enter college, the most striking differences they find from high school are a considerably larger workload and a much greater need to learn effectively on their own. Some students respond well to these challenges, with greater or lesser struggles, and go on to success. Others adjust only to some extent and are hampered throughout their college careers. Still others fail to cope satisfactorily and leave school.

The central value underlying the *hm College Study Skills Program* is that we have a responsibility and an opportunity to help students prepare for college work. The more we can aid them in their development of a repertoire of useful study skills which are appropriate for college level work, the more prepared they will be and, thus, the more successful they will be in college. When students develop a repertoire of study skills, they become both more *independent* as learners and more *efficient* in their learning.

Mastering and using study skills give students a sense of empowerment, of being capable. And that experience of capability breeds a sense of confidence in their own ability to learn, understand, and succeed. When we engage students towards the end of high school or during their first semester in college in the learning and use of college study skills, we can contribute to their potential for empowerment and success as learners both in college and throughout their lives.

THE hm COLLEGE STUDY SKILLS PROGRAM

The *hm College Study Skills Program* is designed to provide *an introduction to the study skills needed for college work* for students in grades 11–13.

The *hm Program* includes 12 activity-oriented units and an Introduction which is itself an activity. Most of the units require from 70–100 minutes of instructional time.

The *hm Program* is structured on the assumption that activity-oriented lessons are a most effective way to teach study skills; more succinctly, that "learning by doing" is the best way to master skills. The program is also based on the values below:

1. Study skills are skills for learning, information-processing procedures which facilitate the learning, retention, and application of knowledge and skill.

2. Study skills are as basic and important as any skills which we can teach in schools.

3. Learning by doing is the only effective way to learn study skills.

4. An important aspect of learning study skills involves learning more about how one learns, that is, one's learning style. Instruction in study skills engages the student in an active participation in her or his own learning. The student is encouraged and provided with the opportunity to develop the ability to exercise his or her own judgment in relation to learning.

5. A considerable part of study skills instruction ought to take place in structured school settings. Whenever possible, study skills instruction should be integrated with the regular curriculum of a class or course. (When this is not possible, study skills teaching and learning should at least be tied to the student's regular course work.)

6. The learning of study skills offers the potential for a transfer effect: a study skill learned in one context may be used in many others.

7. The work of various developmental psychologists, particularly Piaget, has shown us that there is a continuum of cognitive development throughout the years of childhood and adolescence. It is crucial to relate these insights to the teaching of study skills and to ask a student to learn only what is within the realm of her or his developmental level.

The *hm Program* is deliberately designed to address a wide range of student needs, allow for the participation of students with a diversity of skills, and promote learning on various levels of competence.

The *hm Program* includes the following units:

Introduction To Study Skills And Learning Style
I. Listening Is Tuning In
II. Taking Notes Is A College Survival Skill
III. Learning To Survey
IV. Thinking About New Words
V. Asking Useful Questions
VI. Learning From Your Reading
VII. Taking Charge Of Your Learning
VIII. Understanding And Improving Your Memory
IX. Reading Flexibly
X. Gaining From Discussions
XI. Learning From Visuals
XII. Preparing For And Taking Exams

USING THE hm COLLEGE STUDY SKILLS PROGRAM: WHERE AND WHEN

Our classroom testing has shown that the *hm College Study Skills Program* is effective and valuable both at the high school and college levels.

In high school, the *hm Program* can be integrated into an existing 12th grade course or group of courses. (Some schools have also used the *Program* with 11th graders of high ability.) We suggest that you may want to teach the *Study Skills Program* during the second semester of the senior year when students know they are college bound and have already turned their attention in that direction.

If you choose not to integrate the *hm Program* into an existing course, it can still be used, although we believe it will be less effective. If you use the *hm Program* in a separate setting, be sure to have students work with their assignments from their regular courses in the context of their learning about study skills.

In college, the *hm Study Skills Program* can be integrated into an existing course. Or, the *hm Program* may be taught in a "learning skills" or "learning assistance" setting. If you use the *Program* in this way, be sure to have students bring their actual course work into your class and begin to apply the study skills they learn from the *hm Program* to that work.

In college or high school, learning new skills requires time and practice. People learn skills through processes of repeated trial and error. We try a new skill, make mistakes, identify and learn from our mistakes, and then correct them. The *hm College Study Skills Program* provides only one practice for each skill which it introduces. If your students are to master the various study skills presented here, it is essential that you provide them with and/or guide them to opportunities for practice of the study skills.

Given this need for trial and error practice, we suggest that you introduce at most only one unit each week.

SUGGESTIONS FOR TEACHING THE hm COLLEGE STUDY SKILLS PROGRAM

The *hm College Study Skills Program* is designed to be taught by an instructor working with a group of students. The *Program* can be used effectively with classes or groups as small as five or six.

Suggested Directions

The Instructor's Guide offers "Suggested Directions" for teaching each unit in the *Program*. Our classroom testing has shown these methods to be useful. Of course, we invite you to adapt them in ways which you see fit.

We suggest that you examine both the Student Text and the Instructor's Guide carefully prior to your teaching of the various units.

Suggested Times

Each section within the "Suggested Directions" includes approximate times for the activities in that section. Most of the units range from 70–100 minutes. To save class time, you may want to assign sections of some units for homework.

We caution you that these times are approximate. Our classroom testing has shown us that the wide variation in teaching styles results in an equally wide range in the pacing of instruction. We strongly suggest that you examine the units carefully and gauge your planning of instructional time according to your knowledge of how things work in your classroom.

Introduction To The Student Text

Note that the "Introduction To Study Skills" in the student text is an activity-oriented unit in itself. It introduces students to the concepts of study skills and learning style and the relationship between them.

This "Introduction" is actually the first unit in the book and should be taught as any other unit.

Unit Summaries

Each unit includes a summary at the end. While the use of these summaries has not been formally integrated into the "Suggested Directions" for instruction, we recommend that you bring the summaries to the attention of your students.

You will also find each summary included with its unit in the Instructor's Guide.

Learning Study Skills On Your Own

At the end of each unit, students will find a brief section entitled "Learning Study Skills On Your Own." These resources are designed to give students an opportunity to explore their own learning and study skills independently. Each section gives an introduction to a skill or concept and directions through which to pursue it.

You may want to call your students' attention to these resources.

Extension Activities

Each unit includes a list of "Extension Activities" which provide you with many ideas for further instruction in all of the study skill areas included in the *hm Program*.

TEACHING THE hm COLLEGE STUDY SKILLS PROGRAM: IMPORTANT ISSUES

Learning Style

An awareness of and sensitivity to individual learning style differences is one of the central values in the *hm College Study Skills Program*. Students are introduced to the concept of learning style and work with it in a variety of ways throughout the *Program*.

If you are not familiar with recent work in the learning style field, we suggest that you examine *Student Learning Styles: Diagnosing and Prescribing Programs* (Reston, Virginia: National Association of Secondary School Principals, 1979) as a first step in your own education about learning style. Once you've read this collection of articles, you will have many directions which you can then pursue.

Small Groups

For many of the activities in the *hm Program,* we suggest that students work in pairs or small groups. The interaction of students working on a common task can facilitate the learning of skills through shared problem solving.

Small group processes offer a superb method for genuinely engaging students in an activity. Such processes help both to enhance motivation for learning and to increase interest in the content of the lesson, as they offer active participation to each and every student.

Small groups also provide students with a forum where they can discuss their learning with a minimum of risk.

Individual Work in Study Skills

Individual work is of critical importance to the learning of skills. When a study skill is introduced in a group setting, it becomes crucial to provide individual work with that skill through homework and/or other class activities.

Student Perceptions and Expectations

Sometimes students perceive new study skills as more time consuming than their unskilled learning behaviors. In a few cases, this is an accurate perception, but most often it is not.

You can help students gain a wider perspective about their own learning by telling them that any skill, by its very nature, takes more time to use when you are first learning how to do it. Then, as you become more competent in using the skill, it takes less and less time. Ask students to think of examples of this from their own experience. Or, give them a few examples which will illustrate this relationship between competence and time.

Grading

If you teach in an environment where students will only attend seriously to that which is graded, that is, to that which "counts," then we suggest that you grade study skills work in some fair and concrete manner. Your standard of evaluation ought to keep in mind how study skills are learned, namely through repeated practice over time, and set reasonable levels of expected mastery.

If you do not need to grade students' work to encourage their serious participation in the units of the *hm Program,* then we see no reason to do so.

OTHER hm STUDY SKILLS PROGRAMS

The **hm Study Skills Program Level A** . . . . for grades 1-2
The **hm Study Skills Program Level B** . . . . for grades 3-4
The **hm Study Skills Program Level I** . . . . for grades 5-7
The **hm Study Skills Program Level II** . . . . for grades 8-10
The **hm Study Skills Program Level III** . . . . for grades 11-13
The **hm Math Study Skills Program** . . . . for grades 6-10
The **hm Science Study Skills Program** . . . . for grades 7-10
The **hm GED/Adult Learning Study Skills Program** . . . . for Adults

TEACHING THE INTRODUCTION
TO THE STUDENT TEXT

The introduction to the Student Text is designed to provide your students with an initial understanding of what study skills are and what their value can be. It also offers them a first look at the concept of learning style, how this concept relates to their own experience of learning, and how an awareness of learning style can help them learn and use study skills.

If you are interested in understanding more about learning style, you can find a good introduction to the topic in *Student Learning Styles: Diagnosing and Prescribing Programs* (Reston, Virginia: National Association of Secondary School Principals, 1979.)

Suggested Directions for the Introduction

1. Give your students an overview of the Study Skills Program and how you will ask them to use it (what it covers; what value you see in it; how you plan to employ it in class; how you will evaluate their work; etc.). Then, pass out the Student Texts and ask your students to read the "Introduction To Study Skills" (page 1 in the Student Text). Discuss for emphasis as needed.

Suggested time: 8 minutes

2. Organize your students into small groups. Ask your students to read "How Do You Learn?" (page 2 in the Student Text) and answer the question at the end individually. When they are done, have them share their responses within their groups. Then, discuss the variety of responses with the whole class.

Emphasize at the start of this exercise that there is no "right answer," that different ways of learning can be equally effective. Or, you may wish to lead the discussion to that kind of conclusion at the end of the exercise.

10 minutes

3. Have your students read "Learning Style" (page 2) and respond to the question at the end. When they are done, ask them to share their descriptions in small groups.

10 minutes

4. Ask your students to read "More About Learning Style" (page 3) and answer the question at the end. Discuss with the whole group for emphasis as you see fit.

8 minutes

5. Have your students read and complete "Study Skills And Learning Style" (page 4). Discuss.

8 minutes

UNIT I: LISTENING IS TUNING IN

The lecture is still the most common method of instruction in college classes. Yet many, if not most, incoming freshmen lack the necessary listening skills for learning effectively in this kind of classroom.

The purpose of this unit is to introduce the student to the idea of listening as a meaning-seeking activity which requires skillful behavior. The unit provides the student with five specific listening skills which she or he can learn, practice, and use.

> *Please note:* You may want to use Extension Activity #1 (page 14) as an introductory exercise for this unit.

FOR PRACTICES 2, 5, AND 6 IN THIS UNIT, YOU WILL NEED TO PRESENT SHORT LECTURES (3–6 MINUTES) TO YOUR STUDENTS. We suggest that you construct and deliver lectures which are an integral part of your course or class work. We have included three "sample lectures" in the Answer section in this unit. Use these if you wish.

Suggested Directions for Unit I

1. Ask your students to read "Listening Is A Skill" (page 5). Discuss briefly if useful.

    Practice 1 (page 5) is designed to help your students become more aware of how difficult listening can be. First, have them read the directions for this practice. Then, read the following passage aloud only *once.*

    > Along the shore line waves sometimes cut a notch into the nearly vertical side of a *sea cliff.* The segment of shore which slopes gently in a seaward direction is called a *wave-cut terrace.* As the sea cliff is eroded by the ocean waves, rock debris is formed which eventually lodges beyond the terrace. In this way a structure called a *wave-built terrace* is constructed from the rock fragments on the seaward side beyond the terrace.

    Ask your students to label the following features on their diagrams. Many of them will not be able to label more than two.

    sea level   wave-cut terrace   wave-built terrace   sea cliff

    Go over the diagram. Then, discuss your students' experience of listening with a focus on what factors made the task difficult, i.e., lack of context; unfamiliarity with terms; ineffective listening skills, etc.

    Approximate time: 8 minutes

2. Have your students read "Learning To Tune In" (page 5) and "Active Listening" (pages 5–6). Discuss each skill briefly for emphasis.

    Approximate time: 10 minutes

3. Ask your students to read the directions for Practice 2 (page 6). Present a short lecture (3–6 minutes), and give them time to describe its organization. First, discuss with your students their experience of trying to use listening skills #1 and #2. Then, have several students share their descriptions of the lecture's organization and discuss the descriptions' nature and agreement or variation.

Approximate time: 10 minutes

4. Have your students read "Patterns of Organization" (page 7) and the directions for Practice 3 (pages 7–8). Have your students complete Practice 3. Then, have several students read their examples aloud (be sure they're not in the order given), and ask the class to guess the pattern. When you've done enough examples, ask your students to read the directions for Practice 4 (page 8) and complete the practice. Go over it.

You may wish to give your students the opportunity to complete Practices 3 and 4 in pairs.

Approximate time: 10 minutes

5. Have your students read the instructions for Practice 5 (page 9). Let them know that they may take notes in any way which works for them. Present a short lecture (3–6 minutes). Then, have your students share their notes with each other in small groups. Or, have several students write their notes on the board and discuss them. Discuss the ways in which the activity of note taking promotes effective listening.

Approximate time: 10 minutes

6. Ask your students to read the instructions for Practice 6 (page 10). Present the lecture. Then, give your students time to write down the main idea(s) and their evaluations. When they are done, first discuss your student's experience of trying to use skill #4. Then, discuss the main idea(s) and evaluations with the whole class or in small groups.

You may want to use the Unit I Summary (page 11) as a way of reviewing the ideas and skills introduced in this unit.

Approximate time: 10 minutes

ANSWERS FOR PRACTICES IN UNIT I

Page 5: Practice 1

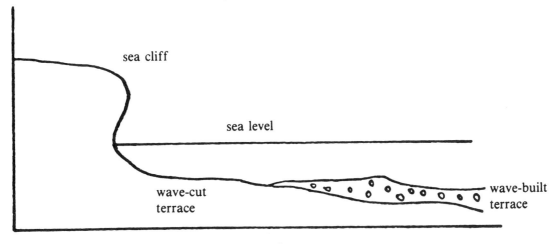

Page 6: Practice 2

Example of a short lecture:

COMPENSATION

What is compensation? In the sense of the word that we are using, compensation refers to behavior which is geared toward making up for a deficiency, real or imagined. Sometimes, with unusual effort, a person can achieve a chosen goal, even if he or she is or feels deficient. In other situations, the person's ability to compensate directs him or her to achieve in another field, often a quite different one.

For example, a person who becomes frustrated in one field — let's say art — may turn to business or a profession as a path to success. In our society, success can come in a variety of ways: through some sort of achievement, through the acquisition of wealth, through the gaining of authority and prestige, through the accomplishment of something unusual, unique, or extremely difficult. Often, though not always, people who succeed in some area do so from a need to compensate for a feeling of deficiency in another area.

Another example is a young man or woman who wants to be a professional athlete. Let's say that person realizes at some point that he or she just doesn't have the ability to make it in pro sports. Then, that person might turn to politics or business as a way of fulfilling what is essentially the same goal: the desire for high level achievement and for the rewards that such achievement brings from fans or voters.

So when we talk about compensation, we mean that a person is making up for a real or felt deficiency of some sort. This sense of overcoming a handicap may be conscious, or it may not be. It may guide our behavior while we're not even aware of it. Whether conscious or not, compensation directs the tension we feel when we are frustrated into some pursuit which is more constructive.

Answers about the organization of the lecture will vary according to what lecture you use. "Compensation" is a definition with examples.

Pages 7–8: Practice 3

The examples which your students write will vary.
1. list
2. cause/effect
3. comparison/contrast
4. sequence/time
5. description or narration
6. definition

Page 8: Practice 4

Accept any reasonable answer.

1.	list	*six . . . truths*
2.	definition	*mean*
3.	comparison/contrast	*distinguish . . . from*
4.	cause/effect	*how . . . occur*
5.	narrative	the entire sentence
6.	sequence	*trace the events*
7.	description	*look in detail*

Page 9: Practice 5

Example of a short lecture:

REQUIREMENTS FOR ECONOMIC GROWTH

The United States has five requirements for economic growth.

First, it needs natural resources. Some of these raw materials from nature, such as land, are limited. Others, like coal, exist in relatively limited quantities and must be preserved or stretched to last at least until acceptable substitutes or synthetics are found. Raw materials like timber are relatively unlimited as long as we keep replacing them.

Another factor in economic growth is labor. It's not enough, however, just to have people available. The people must be skilled and flexible enough to work where they are needed. Some workers must be highly educated to occupy the so-called "white collar" or professional jobs.

Capital, the material wealth we use to produce more wealth, is a critical factor in economic growth. There are three kinds of capital goods. One is the buildings in which business and production take place. The second is the equipment and machinery needed for production. And the third is inventory, or stock on hand, such as materials used for production and the finished products themselves.

Without the fourth factor, technology, an industrial country like the U.S. would be economically backward. Technology helps to combine the natural resources, the laborers, and the capital to increase production. New inventions, new processes, and advances in the old ones expand economic growth.

The last factor, management and ownership, gives focus and direction to the first four. The manager or owner makes decisions affecting the "what" and "how" of production.

Although other factors are involved in economic growth, these five are the most important.

Suggested answer. (Notes will vary. Accept any that are inclusive and make sense to the note taker.)

Requirements for Economic Growth

5 req.
1. Natural res.
   - limited, e.g., land
   - relativ. limited, e.g., coal   Must preserve or find substit. or syn.
   - relativ. unlimited, e.g., timber   Must replace
2. Labor
   - skilled
   - flex.
   - some highly ed.
3. Capital — material wealth that produces more weal.
   - buildings
   - equip. & machin.
   - inventory & products
4. Technology
   - combines 3 above
   - net inventions & processes, advances
5. Mgt. & ownership
   - gives focus to 4 above
   - makes decisions

ANALYSIS

Pattern of organization: A LIST of factors necessary for economic growth. Could also be thought of as CAUSES of economic growth.

Students should list the 5 factors and at least the 3 sub-points under "capital."

Page 10: Practice 6

Example of a lecture:

WHY COAL IS BEING RECONSIDERED

A few years ago, coal was on its way out as an energy source. Today, however, the door has been reopened allowing coal to reenter the energy marketplace. Why has this occurred?

One reason for the return of coal is a newly designed boiler which makes coal burn cleaner. In the new boiler, coal is mixed and burned with particles of limestone. The limestone absorbs 95% of the noxious sulfur and nitrous oxide pollutants. This boiler is so clean that people who suffer respiratory ailments will not be affected by the burning of coal.

Also, the rise of oil prices has made the burning of coal both necessary and feasible. New coal boilers are being produced, whereas a few years ago, when oil was plentiful, they would have been nearly impossible to buy even if someone had wanted to burn coal. Use of solar power and fusion is still decades away, making coal the logical alternative to oil.

Another reason the country is returning to coal is availability. Large coal reserves — more than 200 years worth — exist in the United States. To reach the reserves we must be willing to dig deep and to strip mine. But, in many areas, such methods of extraction are being used in conjunction with restoration of the environment after the mining has been completed.

Government encouragement of the use of coal as an alternative energy source is a fourth reason for its new popularity. Many public buildings have been granted Department of Energy grants to convert to coal. Also, government agencies have been converting on their own.

A final reason for the switch back to coal is the fact that new coal boilers are easy to maintain. A custodian doesn't need a degree in engineering to run one. And the new boilers can be run with fewer personnel than were formerly needed.

In sum, then, coal is making a comeback because of new cleaner boilers, the rise of oil prices, the potential availability of coal for many years, government encouragement of its use, and ease of running a coal burning system.

Suggested Answer. (Notes will vary. Accept any which are inclusive and make sense to the note taker.)

Why Coal Is Being Reconsidered

Reasons
1. New boiler
    limestone particles w. coal
    95% sulfur and nitrous oxide removed
2. Rise of oil prices
    boiler being produced
    solar and fusion — long way off
3. Available
    200+ yrs. reserve
    dig deep, strip mine, restore envir.
4. Gov't encouragement
    DOE grants
    gov't buildings
5. New coal boilers easier to maintain
    less tech. skill
    fewer personnel

ANALYSIS
    Pattern of organization: Better answer is CAUSE/EFFECT. It is also a LIST of the
    reasons (CAUSES) why coal is being reconsidered.
    Key words to C/E pattern: *why, reasons, because*

    Some students will write only the 5 main points. For certain courses this would be sufficient; for others supporting details would be necessary.

EXTENSION ACTIVITIES

1. This is a good motivating activity, one which encourages close listening. Have students listen to the mystery printed below and try to answer the question asked at the end of it.

READ TO STUDENTS

The police already knew where to look for Pete's dead body. A reliable informant said she saw Pete shot in the head and his dead body dumped over the bridge railing into the river. That was four days ago on Monday, but Pete's body had not yet come to shore.

Then Friday morning Detective Supersleuth was called by the police in the next town because they found a body washed up on the muddy river bank. He drove to the spot and examined the remains.

"A terrible sight Pete is," thought Supersleuth, as he studied the pale, watersoaked body with its head shattered and bleeding. He found no identification but only papers too waterlogged to be deciphered without help from the lab. Still, he was sure the body was that of Pete. The size, hair color, and general description fit.

Back at the station Supersleuth told the Captain of his discovery. Supersleuth was shocked when the Captain shouted at him: "You idiot; that can't be Pete's body! I ought to take your badge away!"

How did the Captain know Detective Supersleuth was wrong in his identification?

ANSWER: Pete's been dead four days so it can't be his body with the head bleeding.

2. Have a small group write a biased lecture and give it to the class. Discuss the role of bias in making one "deaf" to the message. How can students learn to "hold fire" in order to hear the points of the speaker even when they strongly disagree with the speaker? Discuss these ideas.

3. Have students list words/ideas that are negative to them, e.g., finish your paper, clean your room, etc. Would they have trouble "hearing" a lecture relating to the above? How could they listen to such a lecture if they wanted to do so? Discuss.

4. Give a lecture allowing many distractions — noise, talking, door opening and closing, etc. See who in the class gets the most important information. Discuss resisting distractions — how to concentrate, move near speaker, etc.

5. Give a lecture or have students watch a videotaped lecture or news broadcast. Ask them to write down the "body language" of the lecturer or newscaster that signals important points.

6. After a lecture or discussion, have students review by telling the main ideas and important details from memory. This constitutes the *review* and making a *whole* of the lecture.

7. Have students listen to a sequence of 4-6 happenings. Ask them to try to remember and recite all of them in order. Work in teams. Try this in conjunction with content area reviews.

8. Prepare some cause/effect statements. The speaker reads one half of a statement. The listener finishes by adding the other half. This can also be done with comparison/contrast. Work in pairs or teams and switch roles.

   CAUSE/EFFECT:
   A. It was snowing heavily. Therefore we . . .
   B. Fruit contains a lot of vitamin C. It should be . . .
   C. The store owner put a cheaper price on the fruit because . . .
   D. All the buildings in the city lay in ruins as a result of . . .

   COMPARISON/CONTRAST:
   A. Sports are fun, but school is . . .
   B. Russia's government is totalitarian, whereas ours is . . .

9. Have students listen to paragraphs on tape which include a part that is illogical or non-sensical. They must explain what doesn't make sense and why.

10. Have students listen to a story or article and predict the ending.

11. Ask students to read a story and then have groups of three students tell their own story similar in theme and language.

12. Tape news commentaries, advertisements, or public opinion broadcasts. Let students try to detect bias and language contributing to bias.

13. Read short news articles and have students write an appropriate headline for each. These articles may be taped. Students may work in teams with the teacher as judge.

14. Ask students to draw an imaginary vehicle — anything that could move a person from place to place. It should be of a kind that the student has never seen before. All students draw their vehicles on 8½ x 11" paper using pencil. One student's drawing is chosen; the student describes it and others try to draw the vehicle, using only the verbal description as a guide.

    Or, have each student describe his/her drawing in words and exchange the description with another student. Students draw according to the description and compare with the original drawing.

15. Lecture, talk, or read and ask students to listen carefully because they will be expected to:

    A. Answer *who, what, when, where, why,* or *how* questions
    B. Give a summary
    C. Act out the story
    D. Tell events or steps in order
    E. Draw a picture of the event, object, setting, etc.

16. Have students think of a typical school day and estimate the number of hours they spend reading — books, newspapers, work forms, etc. Then ask them to estimate the number of hours they spend listening — to parents and siblings, to instructors, to friends, in class, to TV, on the telephone, etc. Now ask them to compare the amount of time reading with the amount of time listening. Discuss.

UNIT I SUMMARY: LISTENING IS TUNING IN

Listening means choosing to focus your attention on what you are hearing. It also means knowing what you've heard and trying to make sense of it.

Listening is an active, meaning-seeking process. A skillful and effective listener is an active listener.

You can become more active as a listener by using these five skills:

1. Choose to tune in to what you are hearing. Tell yourself ''I'm awake and alert, and I'm choosing to listen carefully'' when you begin to listen or when you find your attention drifting.

2. Try to figure out how the presentation you are hearing is organized. Then, use your understanding of that organization to guide your listening.

   Six common patterns of organization are: description or narration
   cause/effect
   comparison/contrast
   definition
   list
   sequence/time

3. When you need to remember what you are hearing, take notes about it.

4. While you listen, ask yourself questions about what the speaker is saying.

5. Try to make a whole message of what you have heard. Then, evaluate it.

UNIT II: TAKING NOTES IS A COLLEGE SURVIVAL SKILL

This unit focuses on the necessity for taking useful notes in college and presents four different methods for note taking. The activities of the unit are designed to help students learn about a variety of note taking methods and about how to use these methods wisely, given their own learning styles and learning needs.

Of course, doing only this unit will not guarantee that students will achieve mastery in any of these skills. To achieve even initial competence, students need ongoing practice with the note taking methods of their choice.

Suggested Directions for Unit II

1. Organize your students into pairs. Tell them that you will ask them to do much of this unit collaboratively.

2. Ask your students to read "Why Take Notes" (page 12) and "How To Take Notes" (page 12). Discuss briefly. Then, have your students read "Outlining" (page 12) and complete Practice 1 (pages 12–13). Ask your students to construct their outlines individually and then compare their outlines with those of their partner. If it seems useful, then go over the outline with the whole class.

Approximate time: 10–12 minutes

3. Ask your students to read "Using A Diagram" (page 13) and to complete Practice 2 (page 13). Ask them this time to work collaboratively on their notes. When they are done, have 2–3 pairs put their notes on the board. Compare the notes and discuss.

Approximate time: 10 minutes

PLEASE NOTE: An important issue in teaching note taking will probably surface at some point during this unit. This issue is the tension between the idea that there is a "correct" set of notes and the idea that notes should vary according to the needs of the learner. Clearly some notes for a particular body of material can be better than others, that is, more accurate, clear, and complete. At the same time, it's helpful to keep in mind that students' needs in note taking will indeed vary.

We suggest that you address this tension when it arises. You can do this by informing students that a set of notes can be evaluated in two ways: (1) how well they represent the material covered; (2) how helpful they are to the learning of a particular student. Another way to speak to this issue is to suggest that two different sets of notes for a particular material can be equally "correct."

17

4. Have your students read "Mapping" (page 14). Discuss briefly. Then, ask them to complete Practice 3 (pages 14–15) collaboratively. When they have done so, have a few pairs put their notes on the board. Compare notes and discuss.

Approximate time: 20 minutes

5. Ask your students to read "Using A Summary" (page 16) and do Practice 4 (page 16) individually. When they are done, ask them to compare their summaries with those of their partner. Then, ask a few students to read their summaries aloud. Discuss.

Approximate time: 10 minutes

6. Have your students read "Finding Your Own Style" (page 16) and "Thinking About Note Taking Style" (page 16). Ask your students to share their preferences in note taking methods with their partners. Then, discuss. (You may want to try an exercise in which students physically group themselves according to note taking preference and talk for a few minutes about learning style and taking notes within these groups. Then, engage the class in a discussion about what they have generated in their small groups.)

Approximate time: 8 minutes

7. Ask your students to read "Listening And Taking Notes" (page 17). Discuss briefly. Then, have your students read the directions for Practice 5 (page 17). PLEASE NOTE THAT FOR PRACTICE 5 YOU WILL NEED TO PREPARE A SHORT LECTURE OF 6–12 MINUTES IN LENGTH. Or, use the "sample lecture" at the end of the Answer section. When your students have reviewed the listening skills in Unit I, deliver the lecture so they can practice listening and taking notes. Then, have them share their notes in small groups. If it is useful, discuss with the whole class.

Approximate time: 15–20 minutes

ANSWERS FOR PRACTICES IN UNIT II

Page 13: Practice 1

CHANGING TRADE PATTERNS

I. Late medieval and early Renaissance trade patterns
   A. Asiatic
   B. Mediterranean
   C. Baltic/England
   D. Overlap areas
      1. Netherlands
      2. Near East
II. Mediterranean, center to world trade
   A. Interregional trade
   B. Banking houses

Page 13: Practice 2

Changing Trade Patterns

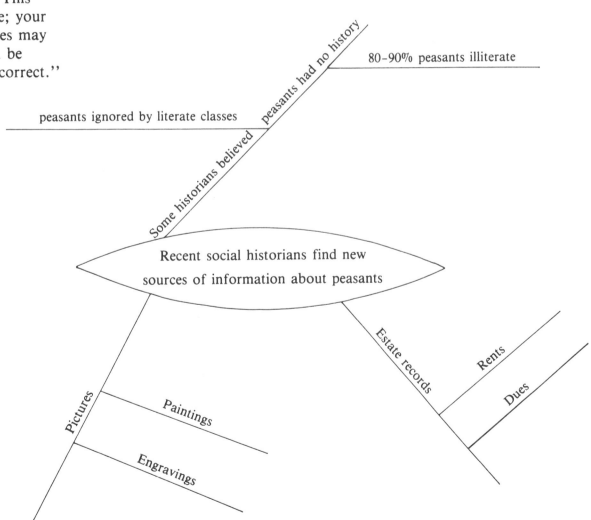

Banking houses

Interregional trade

Baltic/England

Mediter-ranean

Asiatic

Netherlands   Near East

Page 15: Practice 3

THE HISTORICAL SOURCES
(early modern through 18th century)

Please note: This is an example; your students' notes may vary and still be useful and "correct."

80-90% peasants illiterate

peasants had no history

peasants ignored by literate classes

Some historians believed

Recent social historians find new sources of information about peasants

Estate records

Rents

Dues

Pictures

Paintings

Engravings

19

Page 16: Practice 4

An example of a summary:

HISTORICAL SOURCES

Some historians thought that the history of the common people in Europe could not be told because most peasants were illiterate and left no records. Recent social historians have found new sources of information about peasants' lives, such as paintings, engravings, and estate records.

Page 17: Practice 5

Example of a lecture:

THE DISCOVERY OF RADIOACTIVITY

Few scientific discoveries occur suddenly and unexpectedly; rather, they come about through the dedicated efforts of several people over long periods of time. The discovery of radioactivity resulted from many years of persistent investigation.

In 1895 Wilhelm Roentgen observed that cathode rays in a tube from which all air had been evacuated caused certain substances to fluoresce or glow. To study this phenomenon he darkened his lab and wrapped his cathode ray tube in black cardboard. When he looked away from the tube across the room, he noticed that some chemically treated paper glowed when the electricity in the tube was turned on. He reasoned that when cathode rays hit the anode, other unknown rays were emitted that could penetrate solid substances like cardboard, glass, and even walls of a room. Because the nature of these rays was unknown, Roentgen called them x-rays.

Antoine Becquerel took the next step in the discovery of radioactivity when in 1896 he began to study materials that fluoresced in sunlight. He covered a photographic plate with black paper, placed a bit of fluorescent uranium substance on top, and put it in sunlight. Ordinary light couldn't pass through the black paper, but x-rays could. And they affected the film. Next, he noticed that even when the uranium substance wasn't exposed to sunlight, the film still fogged. From this he realized that whatever fogged the film was spontaneously emitted from the uranium substance. He had discovered something more powerful than x-rays — radioactivity.

Beginning in 1898 Pierre Curie, who once worked with Becquerel, and his wife Marie set out to further investigate substances which she termed "radioactive." After four years' effort, in 1902, they reduced a ton of pitchblende into a fraction of an ounce of a substance 400 times more radioactive than uranium. They called the newly discovered, powerfully radioactive element polonium. Later that year they also isolated radium from the pitchblende. The radium, too, was more powerful than uranium.

In 1903 the Curies and Becquerel shared the Nobel Prize for the discovery of radioactivity.

Suggested answer. (Notes will vary. Accept any which are inclusive and make sense to the note taker.)

The Discovery of Radioactivity

The disc. of radioactivity took many yrs.
    1895 Roentgen
       - cathode rays in empty tube fluoresced
       - wrapped tube in black cardboard & across rm. chem. paper glowed when elect.
         on
       - when cath. rays hit anode, unknown rays penetrated cardboard, etc.
       - called x-rays
    1896 Becquerel
       - materials fluor. in sun
       - covered photo. plate w. black paper, put fluor. uranium on top & put in sun
       - sun couldn't pass thru paper but x-rays fogged film
       - even w. no sun film fogged
       - thus uran. emits something more power. than x-rays — radioactivity
    1898 - Curies invest. what Marie called "radioactive" substances
       - 1902 reduced pitchblende & disc. polonium — 400 times more radioact. than
         uran.
         same yr. disc. radium — also more radio. than uran.
    1903 Curies and Becquerel shared Nobel Prize — dis. radioact.

ANALYSIS
    Pattern of organization: TIME or SEQUENCE — the discoveries, in order, leading up
    to the discovery of radioactivity. Some *cause/effect*.
    Note dates.

    Notes should include discovery, date, name. Discovery should be briefly, but
    clearly, explained.

NOTES ABOUT NOTE TAKING

Outlining

Outlines help students to see the organization and interrelation of major and minor topics within a text, lecture, or discussion. This unit teaches the traditional form of outlining. You may want to introduce your students to a less formal outline pattern like the one below:

    A. Main topic
       - Important detail
       - Important detail
          - Minor detail
          - Minor detail

    B. Main topic

21

Diagramming and Mapping

Diagramming is a pictorial way of taking notes. Mapping is a specific form of diagramming which we have found to be highly effective in two ways:

1. For use by students who tend to be visually oriented and have difficulty in outlining.

2. For use in learning situations where the presentation lacks a clear organization or where the organization of the material emerges throughout the process; for example, during a class discussion.

We have also found that mapping has two additional benefits for some students:

1. Students who can visualize effectively, that is, see with their "mind's eye," can see mapping notes, "memorize" them as an image, and recall them through visualization when they so desire.

2. The process of mapping is one of building a structure of knowledge. For many students, this experience leads to a higher degree of active engagement with their learning because mapping is experienced as a creative process.

If mapping is new to you, we suggest that you examine it carefully and experiment with its applications both for yourself and your students.

Help your students master its uses if you share our perception of its value. To learn more about mapping, examine *Using Both Sides Of Your Brain* by Tony Buzan (New York: E. P. Dutton, 1976).

Prerequisites for Outlining and Mapping

Some students have difficulty with note taking because they lack several prerequisite skills for evaluating and organizing ideas and information. These skills include identifying the main idea in a passage, multiple main ideas in a long passage, important details, and necessary minor details.

If your students lack these skills, engage them in appropriate instruction before working with outlining or mapping. For a first practice, choose brief passages of structured material such as a well organized paragraph or section of a chapter. Let students learn to follow the four directions below, starting with step #1 and adding one step at a time.

1. Look or listen for the main idea of the passage.

2. Look or listen for more than one main idea if the passage is long.

3. Look or listen for important details which support the main ideas.

4. Look or listen for minor details which tell you more about the important details. (Here you must make a decision as to what is worth noting. Think about why you are listening or reading, and then decide how much detail you need to note.)

When the material is read or presented aloud, emphasize the important points and transitional words.

If students are reading the material, double space it if possible and allow them to mark on the paper. Teach students to prepare for taking notes by following these steps:

1. Circle main ideas.
2. Underline important details once.
3. Underline minor details with a broken line.

When the students have completed the listening/reading, engage the class in constructing outline and/or mapping notes on the board. Be sure that their contributions are in their own words and in note, not sentence, form.

EXTENSION ACTIVITIES

1. The best extension for this unit is to have students practice *mapping, outlining,* and *summarizing* sections of their textbook assignments. Give practice to the point of mastery in each of these three types of note taking. Students can then choose their preferred note taking method after they thoroughly understand the benefits and liabilities of each. If two or more students are working on the same assignment, let them compare their results. Some readings may lend themselves to diagramming or other methods of note taking.

2. Systematically teach abbreviations for note taking if your students aren't already aware of them. See the hints below.

SUGGESTED ABBREVIATIONS FOR NOTE TAKING

Teach students some or all of these abbreviations to use when they take notes. Teach a few before each lecture and review frequently. Also, encourage students to generate and use their own abbreviations.

1. **USE A SYMBOL SYSTEM**

&	– and
∴	– therefore
=	– equals; means
≠	– does not equal or does not mean
→	– becomes; leads to; yields
+	– plus
–	– minus
>	– greater than
<	– less than
‖	– parallel
w	– with
w/o	– without
vs	– versus

2. **ELIMINATE LETTERS** such as vowels or final letters

    estmtg – estimating   chem – chemistry
    istpe – isotope   devlpg – developing
    psych – psychology

3. **USE AN APOSTROPHE**   '18 – 1918

4. **ABBREVIATE PLURALS**

    chs – chapters
    gov – governments

5. **USE CAPITAL LETTERS** after first using the term once written out

    F – Sigmund Freud
    NATO – North Atlantic Treaty Organization
    M – monists

6. **OMIT PERIODS**

    NY – N.Y. or New York
    pp – pp. or pages

7. **LEAVE OUT UNIMPORTANT WORDS**

All compounds contain elements in certain definite proportions and in no other combinations, regardless of the conditions under which they were produced.

THE ABOVE STATEMENT IS SHORTENED TO: All compds cont elems in cert def proptns & in no other combs, regdless of condit under wh prodcd.

UNIT II SUMMARY: TAKING NOTES IS A COLLEGE SURVIVAL SKILL

Note taking is one of the most important study skills you'll need to learn in college. When you take notes, you begin to make sense of what you're hearing or reading. Also, your notes are very helpful when you prepare for an exam or test.

There are many effective ways of taking notes. Four of these methods are:

1. Outlining   Write the title above the outline. The main ideas are marked with a Roman numeral and placed farthest to the left. The secondary ideas or sub-topics are indented slightly and marked with a capital letter. Details are indented still further and are marked with regular numbers.

2. Using a diagram   Use lines, circles, squares, and so on to organize information into a diagram or "picture."

3. Mapping   Write the main idea in the center of your page. Draw an oval around it. Write the sub-topics or secondary ideas on lines connected to the oval around the main topic. Write the details on lines connected to the sub-topics to which they are related. Write a title at the top of the map.

4. Using a summary   A summary is a brief version of the original reading, discussion, or lecture. Write a summary in sentences and paragraphs. Use your own words, except for technical terms and quotes.

What's most important in choosing a note taking method(s) is how well it works for you. You may want to learn several ways of taking notes and use different methods in different kinds of learning situations.

UNIT III: LEARNING TO SURVEY

When students learn to survey their reading assignments as a first step in reading, they become more effective as readers and learners. Surveying a book, chapter, or article provides you with a framework with which you can direct your reading. It focuses your attention on the organization of the material and gives you an initial interaction with its main ideas and gist. When you survey an assignment, you can also begin to formulate questions about it which can direct your more careful reading of the material.

In this unit students will practice two chapter surveys and one book survey. You may wish to introduce this unit with an exercise like extension activity #2 in this unit.

PLEASE NOTE: YOU WILL NEED TO SELECT SOME OF THE READING MATERIAL FOR YOUR STUDENTS TO SURVEY IN THIS UNIT. Read the Suggested Directions for details.

Suggested Directions for Unit III

1. Ask your students to read "What Is Surveying?" (page 19). Discuss briefly with an emphasis on these ideas:

    a. Surveying takes time but can help you learn more and, thus, save time in the long run.

    b. Surveying gives you a "skeleton" of the reading material on which to hang the ideas and details in the reading.

    c. Surveying should only take a few minutes.

Approximate time: 5 minutes

2. Have your students read "Surveying A Chapter" (page 19). Go over the four steps and briefly discuss. If you think your students will have difficulty with steps #3 and/or #4, include one or both of the following activities:

    a. Have students turn to page 21. Explain that they will find the headings and sub-headings from a chapter in a psychology text on this page. Let them practice — orally as a class or with a partner — turning a few of the headings and sub-headings into questions.

    b. Have students turn to page 22. With a partner, let them practice explaining parts of the summary to each other. You may want to have some students explain for the whole class. Remind your students that some parts of the summary will probably remain unclear until they read the chapter, that one studies the summary first to learn something, but not everything, about the chapter.

Approximate time: 5–15 minutes

25

3. Ask your students to read the directions for Practice 1 (pages 19–20) and to complete this practice. Allow them to work alone or in pairs. If possible, provide each student with access to a dictionary. When students are done with the practice, go over the answers and discuss as appropriate.

   Approximate time: 15–20 minutes

4. Have your students read "More About Chapter Surveys" (page 23). Discuss.

   Approximate time: 4 minutes

5. SELECT A CHAPTER OR ARTICLE WHICH YOU CAN MAKE AVAILABLE TO EACH STUDENT. For example, you can use a chapter from your text which you have not covered yet. Before class, construct an objective test (for example, a ten item multiple choice quiz) based on this reading material, and duplicate a copy for each student.

   Make sure that each student has a copy of the chapter or article which you have selected. Go over the directions for Practice 2 (page 23), and have your students complete the practice. When they have surveyed for four minutes, administer the "test." Then, go over it and have students correct their own papers.

   Discuss the results and students' experience. Many students will score better than they expected. Discuss how this illustrates the ways in which surveying is a learning experience as well as a first step in reading.

   PLEASE NOTE: Encourage your students to work quickly as they survey. It's important that they complete all of the steps within six minutes or less.

   Approximate time: 15 minutes

6. FOR PRACTICE 3 YOU WILL NEED TO CHOOSE THE BOOK WHICH YOUR STUDENTS WILL SURVEY. Be sure that each student has a copy of the book.

   Ask your students to read "Surveying A Book" (page 23) and do Practice 3 (pages 23–24). Allow them to choose to work alone or with a partner. When they are done, go over the answers. Ask several people to share their learnings as described on page 24.

   Approximate time: 15–20 minutes

7. Have your students read "Reading With Purpose" (page 24). Discuss by asking students to share how they might set purposes for different kinds of reading.

   Approximate time: 5 minutes

ANSWERS FOR PRACTICES IN UNIT III

Pages 19-20: Practice 1

Answers will vary. Below you'll find suggested answers.

Title: It means making the most of your learning.

Four major issues: 1. The structure of an individual's knowledge base and how best to add to it.

2. The way in which learning one set of materials transfers to learning another.

3. The importance of information feedback.

4. Motivational and emotional factors that affect learning efficiency.

Questions 1-4

1.   Computer assisted instruction

2-4.   Answers will vary.

Two questions of your own

Answers will vary.

Pages 23-24: Practice 3

Answers will depend on the book you choose.

EXTENSION ACTIVITIES

1. Ask students this question: "If you could only ask five questions about this chapter as you surveyed, what would those five questions be?" Write the questions on the board and evaluate them.

    This activity will help students learn that:

    A. Five good questions will direct the reading of a chapter to some helpful degree.
    B. Some questions will direct the reading of a chapter better than others because they include more concepts.
    C. Chapter survey time can be shortened by writing fewer but better questions.

2. Relate surveying to remembering. Prove to students that if they have the structure and organization of a survey, they'll remember better. Here's the way to prove it. Give one half of the class written directions for a 10 minute structured survey; give the other half of the class directions to read the chapter for 10 minutes. Ask both groups the same questions at the end of 10 minutes and compare the quality of the answers.

3. Students may also prepare certain book parts for their textbooks that lack those parts.

   For example:

   A. Make a glossary for a chapter or short book. This is an especially good activity to complete for a book with many technical and specialized terms.
   B. Make a bibliography for a chapter or book. If students annotate the bibliography, they'll gain practice surveying many books and articles.
   C. Make an index for a book or chapter. Some students will be able to cross reference the index.

4. Have students survey a chapter for a limited time, such as five minutes, and take another five minutes to list from memory the topics or ideas in the chapter.

5. Use the book survey form in this unit, and ask students to complete a survey of another book that they use for a class. Add these points to a textbook survey:
   A. Sub-title
   B. Typographical aids — chapter headings, sub-headings, boldface type, indenting, underlining, etc.
   C. Visuals — maps, graphs, charts, pictures, etc.

UNIT III SUMMARY: LEARNING TO SURVEY

One of the most useful study skills that you can learn is how to *survey* reading material before you read it carefully. When you survey, you look quickly through the reading material to gain a sense of the gist and organization of the chapter, article, book, etc.

A *chapter survey* gives you a "skeleton" of what the chapter covers. To survey a chapter, read and think about:

> the title
> the introduction
> the headings and sub-headings
> the summary

A *book survey* tells you what the book is about and what parts of the book you can use to help you learn. To survey a book, read and, when appropriate, think about:

> the title
> the author(s)
> the date of publication
> the introduction and/or preface
> the table of contents

Also, find out if the book includes an index, a glossary, or an appendix. Do the chapters in the book have introductions and/or summaries?

You can use your survey of a reading assignment to give purpose(s) to your reading.

UNIT IV: THINKING ABOUT NEW WORDS

This unit involves your students in working with several basic vocabulary acquisition skills. The intent of the unit's activities is to help students discover how they can learn new vocabulary in ways which are an integral part of their reading experience.

Learning vocabulary through context is the most useful skill addressed. It is the most natural way to learn the meaning of new words.

Learning vocabulary through structure is also important. Structural analysis is a huge topic in itself, and the exercises here are designed only to introduce the nature of this skill. Many good sources are available to students and teachers who wish to pursue structural analysis in greater depth.

Use of the dictionary is noted briefly. If your students are not able to use the dictionary effectively, instruction in the use of this tool is essential.

Please note: This unit may be taught as a whole, or you may choose to teach it in parts which are interspersed with later units or with other class work. If the unit is spread out over a long period of time, you may want to review the previous sections with your students before beginning new ones.

Suggested Directions for Unit IV

1. Ask your students to read "Unfamiliar Words: What Do You Do?" (page 26) and answer the question at the end. When they are done, have them share their responses in pairs or small groups. Then, with the whole class, ask students to name the methods they have described while you list them on the board. Continue until you have all of the methods suggested by students on your list.

   You may want to discuss each method briefly. Or, use the list to focus students' attention on context, structure, and the dictionary.

   Approximate time: 10 minutes

2. Have your students read "Learning About Unfamiliar Words" (page 26) and "Using Context" (page 26). Discuss briefly as is useful. You may wish to emphasize the distinction between *context* and *context clue*.

   Approximate time: 5 minutes

3. Ask your students to read "Direct Context" (page 27) and do Practice 1 (pages 27–28) individually or in pairs. (For this practice and any others in the unit, you may wish to go over the first item with the whole class as an example.) When students are done, go over the exercise.

Approximate time: 8 minutes

4. Have students do Practice 2 (page 28), or assign it for homework. If you are working with very able students, you may want to omit Practice 2.

Approximate time: 5 minutes

5. Ask your students to read "Indirect Context" (page 28), and have students do Practice 3 (pages 28–31) in pairs. Then, go over the practice. Have your students complete Practice 4 (page 31) next, and go over it with the whole class.

    Please note: Many students will find indirect context much more difficult than direct context and will need additional practice with this skill.

    You may want to discuss with students the idea that context won't always work and that its usefulness will vary. To learn about this variation and master the basic skills of context, students need the opportunity to practice these skills often, without fear of penalty for wrong answers.

    When your students are learning to use context, ask them to do the best they can without turning to a dictionary.

Approximate time: 15–25 minutes

6. Have your students read "Structure" (page 32), and complete Practices 5–8 (pages 32–33) individually or in pairs. Go over the practices. (If your students have difficulty working with structure, you may wish to have them do the practices one at a time and devote more time to working with each element of structure.)

Approximate time: 10–15 minutes

7. Have your students read "Using Structure" (page 33) and "Context Plus Structure" (page 33). Then, have them do Practice 9 (pages 33–34). Or, assign this practice for homework. At some point, go over the practice and discuss it.

Approximate time: 10 minutes

8. Ask your students to read "Using A Dictionary" (page 34). Discuss as is useful. Then, have your students read "Words As Concepts" (page 35) and discuss.

    Please note: The understanding of words as concepts is critical to effective learning at the college level. We strongly suggest that you provide your students with opportunities to work with this idea. You can find suggestions for such instruction in this unit's Extension Activities.

Approximate time: 5 minutes

ANSWERS FOR PRACTICES IN UNIT IV

Pages 27–28: Practice 1

A. clue — that is   *can be beaten flat without breaking*

B. clue — or, appositive   *ceremony of transition from the child role to the adult role*

C. clue — parentheses   *guardian*

D. clue — dashes   *asked nature direct questions in the form of planned manipulations*

Page 28: Practice 2

1. socialization: process by which children learn the rules and expectations of their culture

2. chemical change: fundamental alteration in the nature and structure of a substance

3. wrought iron: iron in pure form

4. flyboats: ships specially designed with shallow drafts to navigate the shallow coasts and estuaries of the Netherlands

Pages 28–31: Practice 3

A. explanation: We know from our experience that radio broadcasts are usually exactly on time. But this bout could be delayed because it wasn't broadcast on radio.

   punctuality = promptness, quality of being on time

B. explanation: The mood indicates sadness, a weak voice. She was weeping, sobbing, gasping.

   quavering = trembling, shaking

C. explanation: A number of extremely loud machines were all operating at the same time.

   excruciating = causing intense pain

D. explanation: The unknown word is in a series with two synonyms.

   lollygagger: bum, idler

E. explanation: The word "but" shows contrast between his earlier and later moods.

   amiability = friendliness

Page 31: Practice 4

1. ingenuously = simply, innocently
2. misanthropic = unsociable, disliking other people
3. wallowing = rolling about in
   latent = hidden or dormant
4. inarticulately = incoherently, without clear expression
5. incensed = angered greatly

Page 32: Practice 5

1. genocide
2. genetic
3. generation

Page 32: Practice 6

1. homo + cide
2. mater + cide
3. frater + cide
4. homicide, matricide

Page 33: Practice 7

1. regeneration
2. precondition

Page 33:Practice 8

1. genetic
2. genetically
3. generation

Pages 33-34: Practice 9

1. interface = surface (face) forming a common boundary between two bodies
2. equilibrium = state of (equal) balance
   displacement = act of removal
   innovations = new ideas or devices

EXTENSION ACTIVITIES

1. Clip out short articles of approximately the same length (edit if necessary) from magazines and journals, newspapers, etc. Underline 5-10 difficult words. Ask students to skim for 2-3 minutes (allow about 1 minute for each 400-500 words) and then write in one or two sentences what the article was about.

   Next have them figure out the meanings of the underlined words from context. Provide an answer sheet with the main idea and word meanings.

   Students can work in pairs by each completing one article, swapping, comparing answers and then using the answer sheet.

2. Provide students with a chart like the one below, a limited list of prefixes and roots with their meanings, and some pages in a textbook (chapter, section, etc.). Organize students in groups of 2-4 and have them search the chapter and fill in the chart with words whose meanings are unlocked by word structure. Provide each group of students with a collegiate dictionary.

CHART FORM

WORD	PREFIX OR ROOT	MEANING OF PREFIX OR ROOT	MEANING OF WORD

Have students write the word twice or more if it has two or more structural parts.

3. Ask students to watch a television program for ½ hour and listen for 5 unfamiliar words. Ask them to write each word in its context. Have them share some of the words and categorize them by content area.

4. Have students keep a notebook page for each content area and each week add a certain number of words to each list.

5. Practice with new words. Have students prepare at least three slips of paper as shown below for each of 10 words. Write the 10 words on the chalkboard or on cardboard. Have a student teach the meanings and uses of the words to a small group of peers. Then have students practice the words using a method called directed teaching. Directed teaching is done in this manner: A student or instructor reads from a slip of paper, taps a pencil or chalk, and students respond orally with the correct word from the list that fits the context. Work rapidly to complete 30 slips and if necessary mix them up and repeat. For a final activity, have students write the words instead of saying them. Or you may want students to write the words from memory as the context slip is read. This method offers a great deal of practice in a very limited time period.

WORD	CONTEXT SLIPS (3 per word)
erudite	The professor is very _____.
	My friend, who understands literature very well, is _____ in that area.
	She is an educated, learned, and _____ person.

6. Outline vocabulary so students learn interrelationships among words. This forms a basis for learning content vocabulary in an integrated fashion.

EXAMPLE: PROBLEMS OF THE 20s AND 30s (chapter section)
  prohibition
    intoxicating
      distillery
      light/hard
      saloon
      bar
      speakeasy
      inebriated
    dry/wet
    temperance

EXAMPLE: RESTRICTION OF IMMIGRATION (chapter section)
  immigrant
    old
    new
      undesirables
        quota system
        racial stock
        national origins
        aliens
      preferred
        mental fitness
        physical fitness
        literacy
          assimilation
  homogeneous population
  residing
  ports of embarkation
  visa
  tide

The examples above outline new vocabulary and vocabulary used in new ways. Ask students to outline significant words from a chapter and define them after reading. Or have them use the words outlined in a summary/review of the section.

UNIT IV SUMMARY: THINKING ABOUT NEW WORDS

When you come across unfamiliar words in your reading, you need to find out what they mean if you wish to understand what you've read.

One way to define an unfamiliar word is by using its context. *Direct context* means that the unfamiliar word is clearly defined within the text. Several direct context clues are:

    a. words like "is," "that is," "means," etc.

    b. appositives

    c. parentheses

    d. dashes

Indirect context means that the unfamiliar word is only indirectly defined in the text. To use indirect context, you must play an "educated guessing" game using clues such as:

    a. Your own experience

    b. The mood and tone of the passage

    c. Examples of the unknown term

    d. Words in a series which are roughly synonymous with the unknown term

    e. Words with meanings opposite to the unknown term

Another way to learn about the meaning of an unknown word is through its *structure*. With some words you can examine their prefixes, roots, and/or suffixes to help you figure out their meanings.

Sometimes using *context plus structure* can help you to define an unfamiliar word.

If neither context nor structure offer enough information about the meaning of an unfamiliar word, you need to use your dictionary.

When you have learned how to use context, structure, and the dictionary, you'll have gained a repertoire of skills for building your vocabulary.

UNIT V: ASKING USEFUL QUESTIONS

Asking and answering appropriate questions about a reading or lecture is a powerful learning skill which promotes the student's active and focused involvement. Questioning also helps to increase concentration and improve memory.

The purpose of this unit is to introduce your students to the uses of a question-and-answer method in reading and listening. The unit's activities are designed to help students begin to ask useful and appropriate questions.

The skill involved in posing good questions is not an easy one to learn. You may find that your students need a good deal of additional work with this skill before they gain competency in it.

Please Note: FOR PRACTICE 5 IN THIS UNIT, YOU WILL NEED TO DEVELOP AND PRESENT A SHORT LECTURE. Or, use the "Sample Lecture" at the end of the Answer section.

Suggested Directions for Unit V

1. Ask your students to read the "Introduction" (page 37). Discuss as is appropriate. Then, ask your students to read "Literal Questions and Exploratory Questions" (page 37). Explain that literal questions address facts and ideas directly stated, not opinions or judgments. You may wish to have students give some examples of both kinds of questions.

   Approximate time: 8 minutes

2. Have your students complete Practice 1 (pages 37–38), but do not go over it immediately. First, review "Asking Literal Questions" (page 38) with your students, focusing on the three characteristics. Then, ask your students to check their answers to Practice 1 and label the two incorrect choices according to which characteristic(s) of effective literal questions they do not fulfill. When they have done so, go over the practice and discuss each correct and incorrect question.

   Approximate time: 10–15 minutes

3. Have students read "Asking Questions And Reading A Textbook" (page 38). Then, ask them to do Practice 2 (page 39). Go over the practice.

   Approximate time: 8 minutes

4. Ask your students to organize themselves into pairs. Have them read "Writing Your Own Literal Questions" (page 39) and do Practice 3 (pages 39–40) cooperatively. When they are done, go over the practice.

   Students sometimes find this kind of questioning difficult. Suggest that if they can't find a topic sentence, they should look for the "who" or "what" of the paragraph and then determine what the author is saying about the "who" or "what."

   Approximate time: 10 minutes

36

5. Ask your students to read "Asking Exploratory Questions" (page 40). Discuss as is appropriate. Then, have your students read and examine "Asking Questions And Taking Notes" (page 41) and do Practice 4 (pages 42-43) in pairs. When they are done, have several pairs share their notes with the class. Discuss and evaluate the various examples of notes. (Be aware that the format on page 41 encourages question and answer notes.)

Approximate time: 20-30 minutes

6. Ask your students to read "Thinking About Your Questions" (page 44). Discuss as is appropriate. You may want to explain to students that too many questions can be counterproductive. Questions can be used as thinking tools even when they're not written down.

Approximate time: 5 minutes

7. Prepare an 8-10 minute lecture before class, or use the "sample lecture." For Practice 5 (pages 44-45), deliver the lecture as your students take notes. Have students write their notes on the right side of the page as they did in Practice 4. When the lecture is finished, ask students to write appropriate questions on the left side of the page. Ask several students to share their questions and notes with the class. Discuss and evaluate their questions and notes.

Approximate time: 15-20 minutes

ANSWERS FOR PRACTICES IN UNIT V

Pages 37-38: Practice 1

1. **C** is the best answer.

   B does not fulfill characteristics #1 and #2. It does not address the main idea and is not comprehensive.

   A is better than B, but it does not fulfill characteristics #2 and #3.

2. **A** is the best answer.

   B does not fulfill characteristics #1 and #2. However, B is better than C.

   C does not fulfill characteristic #1.

3. **B** is the best answer.

   A and **C** do not fulfill characteristic #1.

Page 39: Practice 2

These are suggested answers. Other good answers are certainly possible.

1. What is (Explain) the photoelectric effect?

2. Define (What is) bullionism.

3. Correct as is

4. What did Pasteur discover about tartaric acid salts?

5. How do covalent bonds hold a water molecule together?

Pages 39–40: Practice 3

These are suggested answers. Other good answers are certainly possible.

1. In what ways did Prince Henry aid Portuguese expansion in the early part of the 15th century?

2. Explain budding.

Pages 42–43: Practice 4

Notes will vary. The key aspect is the usefulness of the questions and answers to the student.

Pages 44–45: Practice 5

Notes will vary as in Practice 4. Below you'll find a sample lecture which you can use.

CHANGES AFTER 1000 A.D.

Some periods in history are static, or relatively without change; other periods are dynamic, or almost continually changing. During the dynamic period that began in Europe during the eleventh century many changes occurred.

Secular, that is, worldly things changed greatly. Towns grew up before people's eyes. Commerce and government began to develop. The population increased steadily in Western Europe until the fourteenth century.

Because life was secure, farmers were able to plant crops and know they would live to enjoy the results. Also, houses were built to be passed down to one's children.

Feudalism added to the stability of the time by creating lord-vassal relationships. The lord protected the vassal and granted him justice and land in return for which the vassal served the lord as a fighting man and sometimes paid the lord fees.

One important aspect of feudalism was its mutual, or "you scratch my back, I'll scratch yours," character. The lord and the vassal, or in another instance, the king and the people, each owed something to one another. From this idea of mutual obligation later grew the idea of a constitutional government.

Under feudalism the manorial system grew. Peasants worked for the lords on the manor or huge estate and, in turn, they were protected and supported. The manor, because it produced an abundance of food and goods, also supported the clergy.

Some changes had already occurred before 1000 A.D. that made subsequent changes possible. Agricultural inventions had increased animal productivity and windmills were being used for power. These earlier inventions virtually eliminated slavery in Europe after 1000 A.D.

An important new change was the move from the "two-field" to the "three-field system" of planting. In the "two-field system" one half the land was planted at one time while the other half rested. In the newer "three-field system" one part was planted with one crop, a second part was planted with another crop, and the third part, only, rested. This greater cultivation, plus better plowing, and more effective use of animals created more food.

One consequence of the food surplus was population growth. Since some of these new people were no longer needed on farms, they moved to populate the new towns.

All these changes and others contributed to the dynamic period that immediately followed 1000 A.D.

EXTENSION ACTIVITIES

1. Have students write questions in the margins of printed material and underline the answers to their questions. Questions should be directed toward main ideas and supporting details.

    STEPS IN UNDERLINING
    A. Read the entire section (or chapter if it is short) before underlining anything.
    B. Underline main ideas, definitions, rules, laws, principles, etc.
    C. Underline only the important supporting ideas.
    D. Underline an example or illustration of the points being made only when you need it for clarification.
    E. Underline just enough words to make sense. Check by rereading the material.

    When students finish the underlining, they phrase broad questions and write them in abbreviated form in the margins. For example, if a section of underlined text described four causes of the Civil War, in the margin students would write: "4 causes Civ. War?" Or for a definition of photosynthesis, they'd write: "photosynthesis?" Often students can rely for help in phrasing questions on chapter sub-headings. If there are no sub-headings, they will have to phrase their own questions.

    To study from in-textbook notes, students cover the text, read the question, try to answer, and finally check against the underlining.

2. Have students listen to very brief lectures or paragraphs read aloud and practice writing questions about them.

3. Have students study the title and introductory paragraph(s) of short stories or novels and pose both literal and exploratory questions that may be answered through reading. This technique is especially helpful because many students pass too quickly over introductory material, wanting to jump right into the plot. One particularly effective vehicle for this technique is Walter Van Tilberg Clark's short story "The Portable Phonograph."

UNIT V SUMMARY: ASKING USEFUL QUESTIONS

Asking and answering questions about what you are studying is a powerful tool for learning.

Asking and answering questions (1) involves you actively in what you are learning, (2) helps you to focus on what's important in what you are studying, and (3) helps you to concentrate and remember more effectively.

Literal questions refer to ideas, concepts, and data which are directly stated in a book, article, or lecture. An effective literal question is comprehensive and clearly expressed. When you read textbooks or articles, you can use titles and headings to help you construct useful literal questions about your reading. Then, read the section below the title or heading so you can answer your question.

When you read printed material without headings or when you listen to a lecture, you need to construct your own questions.

Exploratory questions relate to meanings, implications, and your own interests and curiosity. These questions go beyond what is stated and involve analysis, critical and creative thinking, and discovery.

You can use your questions to help you organize your notes. Use the left side of your paper for questions, the right side for notes which answer the questions, as shown below.

Question I	I. Main idea
	A. Detail
	B. Detail
Question II	II. Main idea
	A. Detail
	1. Sub-detail
	2. Sub-detail
	B. Detail

UNIT VI: LEARNING FROM YOUR READING

As they enter college, many if not most students read assignments in essentially the same way as they did when they began junior high or middle school. This unskilled approach to reading is characterized by the following behaviors:

- The student begins at the first word of the assignment (and often at the first word after the introduction, if there is one) and reads to its conclusion (and often to the last word before the summary, if there is one). In doing so, the student makes little or no use of the material's organizational features to aid her or his learning.

- The student reads passively, without considering the purpose for his or her reading and without actively thinking about the content and implications of the material.

- The student reads through the material only once, often as quickly as possible, without surveying or reviewing.

This unit introduces students to a more skillful, strategic, and effective way of reading assignments and learning from them. It is a direct and relatively simple method for reading based on the need for purpose, activity, and repetition in learning.

As this method stresses the importance of taking appropriate notes, the first part of the unit involves students in working with note taking skills as they apply to print material.

> *Please Note:* The activities of this unit ask your students to use skills to which they were introduced in Units II, III, and V. You may want or need to review these units with your students or to refer your students to them as resources.

Suggested Directions for Unit VI

1. Organize your class into small groups of 3-4. Ask your students to read "How Do You Read?" (page 48) and respond to the question at the end. Ask them to share their responses in their groups and discuss them when all group members have finished writing. After a period of discussion, gather the class as a whole and ask each group to summarize its discussion. See if any norms or generalizations become evident. If so, discuss them.

Approximate time: 8-10 minutes

2. Have your students read "Learning From Your Reading" (page 48), "Taking Notes From Your Reading" (page 49), and "Boiling Down" (page 49). Discuss briefly if useful.

Approximate time: 5 minutes

3. Have your students do Practice 1 (pages 49-52) in pairs (or, if necessary, trios). When both pairs in a group have completed A-D, have them share their responses with each other and discuss. Or, ask your students to do Practice 1 individually and then share their responses with their groups. When students have gone over A-D, ask them to raise any issues, problems, or concerns about note taking which this exercise aroused. Discuss.

Approximate time: 20 minutes

41

4. Ask your students to do Practice 2 (page 53) individually. Then, have several students write their notes on the board. Compare the various notes and discuss their strengths and weaknesses.

    Approximate time: 10-15 minutes

5. Ask your students to read "Reading And Learning: What's Important?" (page 54) and "A Method For Reading And Learning" (pages 54-55). Go over the main points for emphasis, and discuss as is useful. *(Please note: the study method presented here is a variation of SQ3R. It includes a step for **thinking** about your purpose and background. The **questioning** step becomes a part of the **survey**. To **recite**, students take notes.)*

    Approximate time: 8 minutes

6. Have your students do Practice 3 (pages 55-57) in pairs or individually. When they are done, ask them to share their notes with their groups and discuss differences and similarities, strengths and weaknesses.

    Approximate time: 20-30 minutes

7. Ask your students to read "Thinking About How You Read" (page 58) and "A Few More Hints About Taking Notes" (page 58). Discuss as is useful.

    Approximate time: 5 minutes

ANSWERS FOR PRACTICES IN UNIT VI

Please note that the notes below are suggested answers. Other responses may be equally "correct."

Pages 49-59: Practice 1

A. The most important change in late 18th century economic life in England was the quickly rising output of newly industrialized industries.

B.

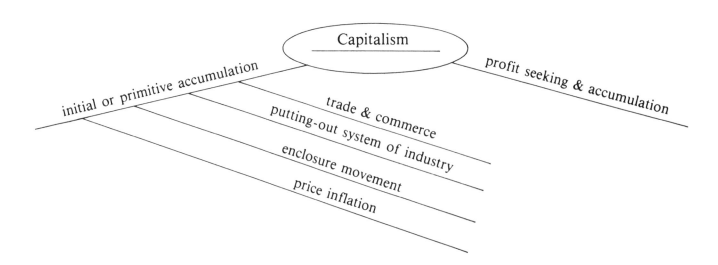

42

C. Features of manorial system

    1. Farmable land in 2 parts, lord's, tenants'

    2. Land cultivated in scattered strips

    3. Tenants worked own and lord's land

D. 1. the thermometer
   2. how a thermometer works

I. Thermometer

    A. Measures hotness, coldness

    B. Uses thermometric (temperature-measuring) property of materials

       1. Thermom prop = different values at diff temperatures

       2. Materials: mercury, gases, metals

Page 53: Practice 2

Failing in math — feels like "sudden death"
                 feels like you can learn no more math, ever
                 not rational, reassurance doesn't help
                 first feel anxiety, then paranoia — fear of being "exposed"

Page 57: Practice 3

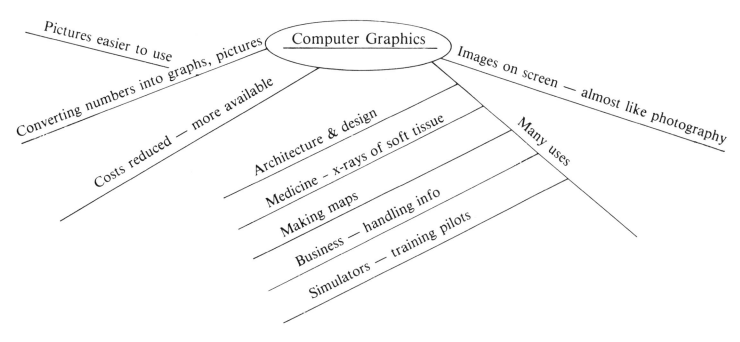

43

EXTENSION ACTIVITIES

1. Give students practice with transitional words and other devices used to indicate changes of direction in prose. Collect many examples of passages in which transitional devices are used. Ask students to circle the devices and discuss how they operate to clarify the ideas in the selection. Below is a list of transitional devices according to category.

TIME or SEQUENCE	next, then 1, 2, A, B, C, I, II, first, second, third, before, since, after, at last, previously, subsequently, now, today, later, soon, finally, etc.
CAUSE/EFFECT	because, thus, for this reason, as a result, if . . . then, since, hence, accordingly, consequently, etc.
COMPARISON/CONTRAST	but, yet, on the other hand, on the contrary, still, though, less, more, however, nevertheless, like, similar to, comparatively, tall*er,* here/there, in contrast, opposite etc.
DEFINITION	is, means, are, is called, or, that is, etc.
ADDITION or LIST	and, plus, in addition to, also, besides, too, one/another, furthermore, moreover, plurals (reason*s,* type*s*)
CLIMAX or CONCLUSION	thus, in summary, in conclusion, finally, for these reasons, in brief, most important, big*gest,* above all, etc.
EXAMPLE or ILLUSTRATION or AMPLIFICATION	for example, let me illustrate, that is, in other words, etc.
TYPOGRAPHY	bold face type, italics, headings and sub-headings, extra white space to set off sections or to indicate change in fiction, colored type, shaded or tinted paper for supplementary material or to highlight very important material, quotations indented and in different type to support the point just made

After students have learned to find and understand the transitional devices, have them use them to help find important points for note taking.

2. Find some book chapters or journal articles that have extra white space between sections. Ask students to read the section and then go back and title it as an editor might. This technique is especially helpful when students take courses with professors who assign several paperbacks. By the time the students have titled each section of a chapter, they have created a very succinct summary of it.

3. Another effective technique for dealing with a multiplicity of course readings is the card technique. Have students read several related articles and fill out a 4 x 6 card for each.

   First, they read the article, making a checkmark in the margin beside each important point. Then, they fill in the front of the card this way:

   ```
   Topic & date:
   Title & author:
   Summary:
   ```

   After a class discussion and further thought about the article, students fill in the back of the card this way:

   ```
   Extra notes from class discussion:
   Definitions & terms:
   Article's relationship to other concepts and readings:
   ```

   Studying from these cards facilitates exam preparation; they're easy to carry around and review.

4. Choose articles and sections from textbooks, and have students take notes on them in one of the ways they learned in this unit.

5. To demonstrate succinct note taking, have students prepare a 100 word (or so) "telegram" of their reading.

UNIT VI SUMMARY: LEARNING FROM YOUR READING

You can learn more effectively from your reading when you use a method which includes:

          PURPOSE   ACTIVITY   REPETITION

This unit presents such a method which has five steps:

Thinking: Before you begin any study, ask yourself what your purpose is. Why are you doing this? What do you want to get from it? What do you already know about the topic?

Surveying: Next, survey what you plan to read to gain a sense of what the main ideas and questions are in the reading.

Reading and
taking notes: Read the material and take useful notes as you go along.

Reviewing: When you've finished reading, take a few minutes to go over your notes and review the main ideas and examples.

An important note taking skill is "boiling down" the meaning or message of a paragraph or passage to its main idea(s). Sometimes this idea(s) can be noted in a few words. When the text is more dense, you usually need to write more in your notes.

UNIT VII: TAKING CHARGE OF YOUR LEARNING

This unit involves your students in a consideration of how they organize their "inner selves" to prepare for and conduct studying. It asks them to reflect on what "being in charge of your own learning" means and in what ways they can take charge.

The unit focuses on three aspects of study behavior: setting goals; creating a helpful study environment; and managing time wisely. Its activities are designed to engage students in introspection in a non-judgmental, non-threatening way and to introduce them to strategies for organizing their goals, study environment, and time more effectively.

One section of this unit also asks your students to view their preferences in study environment as another element of learning style.

Of course, the activities of this unit can only begin the task which they address. You may want to engage your students in more work with these concerns.

Please Note: Students may perceive some of the information which they generate in this unit as private and personal. Please stress right at the beginning of the unit that students need only share with others what they are comfortable in sharing.

Suggested Directions for Unit VII

1. Organize your class into small groups of 3–4.

2. Ask your students to read "Who's In Charge?" (page 60). Discuss as is useful, focusing on the distinction between habit and choice.

   Approximate time: 5 minutes

3. Have your students read "Goal Setting" (page 60) and do Practice 1 (page 60). Ask them to share their goals with their group when everyone in the group is ready. Then, have them read "Setting Realistic Goals" (page 60), and complete Practice 2 (page 61) and Practice 3 (page 61). Ask them to share their responses to the practices in small groups and to discuss what "realistic goals" are.

   Approximate time: 15 minutes

4. Have your students read "Visualizing Your Goals" (page 61) and "When You Don't Succeed" (pages 61–62). Discuss for emphasis, and review the major elements in setting realistic goals.

   Approximate time: 6 minutes

5. Ask your students to read "Your Study Environment" (page 62) and do Practice 4 (page 62). When they are finished, ask them to share their descriptions with their group. Then, have your students complete Practice 5 (pages 62–63), and share and discuss their responses with their group. You may wish to conclude this part of the unit with a whole class discussion focusing on (1) what makes a good study environment for most people, and (2) what kinds of differences in learning style exist in relation to preferred study environment.

   Approximate time: 10–15 minutes

6. Have your students read "Using Your Time Wisely" (page 63). Discuss briefly. Then, ask your students to read "Creating A Schedule" (pages 63–64) and follow the various steps. When students are done, ask them to share their schedules with a partner or with the members of their group. Invite them to give feedback and comments to each other.

Approximate time: 20–25 minutes

7. Ask students to read "Using Your Schedule" (page 67). Discuss as is useful. Encourage them to schedule a second week.

Approximate time: 5 minutes (not including second scheduling)

8. Have students read " 'Stealing' More Time For Study" (page 68) and do Practice 6 (page 68). When students are done, list all the ideas generated on the board or on newsprint, and discuss as is useful. Then, ask students to read "When You Still Need More Time" (page 68). Discuss briefly.

Approximate time: 8 minutes

ANSWERS FOR PRACTICES IN UNIT VII

All answers for practices in Unit VII will vary according to students' learning styles, needs, interests, and so on.

EXTENSION ACTIVITIES

1. One way to help students learn how to take charge of their learning is to initiate a self management project according to the outline below.

    I. State your *goal.*
       EX. To increase your study time.

    II. *Observe and record* the behavior you wish to change.
       EX. Keep a written record for a few days of *when, for how long,* and *under what circumstances* you presently study each day.

    III. State the *exact changes* you plan in your behavior.
       EX. To increase your study time by four hours each week

    IV. *Change the events* that trigger your behavior. You noted these in step II.
       EX. Instead of chatting with friends between classes on Monday, Wednesday, and Friday, plan to go to the library directly from class.
       EX. Bring a specific assignment to complete during time you would otherwise waste.
       EX. Add the 4 hours to your study schedule.
       EX. Turn off the TV because you are easily trapped into watching for two hours when you planned to watch only for one.

    V. Arrange *rewards and punishments* to direct your behavior.
       EX. Think about good grades and other good effects that extra study might bring.
       EX. Plan time out with friends after your goal is met.
       EX. Plan TV time after your goal is met.
       EX. Tell somebody of your intended behavior change and explain your success or failure to that person on a weekly basis.
       EX. Keep a chart of your behavior and mark it regularly.
       EX. Talk to yourself when you sense you are straying from your goal.

    VI. After two or more weeks, compare your behavior with what you observed and recorded in step II. Make further changes if necessary.

2. Allow time for students to prepare their assignment or appointment books. Be sure they plan to enter both regular and long range assignments.

UNIT VII SUMMARY: TAKING CHARGE OF YOUR LEARNING

Who is in charge within you when you want to learn? Do you do things mostly by habit? Or do you choose how and what you intend to learn? The more you can be in charge of your learning and choose what you intend to do, the more successful you'll be as a learner.

You can take more effective charge of your learning by: (1) setting goals for yourself; (2) creating a helpful study environment; and (3) using your time wisely.

Goal Setting

Goals are targets towards which you aim. For goals to be helpful, they must be realistic. A realistic goal is:

        a. Capable of being stated clearly

        b. Believable

        c. Achievable

        d. Measurable

Setting goals helps you figure out what you want and need to accomplish. Working towards the achievement of your goals helps you to organize your energies and work more effectively.

Another way to work with goals is to visualize what success would be. When you see an image of what achieving a particular goal would be, you can use this image to help you know towards what end you are working and to move towards that end.

Study Environment

Another part of your learning style involves your preferred study environment: where and under what conditions you learn best. In what kind of place do you learn best? Using what kind of furniture? Light? Sound? Temperature? What time of day? How much and what kinds of noise/quiet? Before or after meals? And so on.

Examine the environment in which you study now, and try to improve it in any ways that work for you.

Using Your Time Wisely

Using your time wisely means managing your time: figuring out what you want and need to do, and how to do it within the time you have. One helpful tool for managing time is a schedule. Rather than limiting you, a good schedule gives you more choice because it helps you waste less time.

Try creating a week's schedule and using it to see how it can help you manage your time better. Whenever you create a schedule, remember that you are doing this only for yourself. Use the schedule as a tool which helps you accomplish the goals you've set for yourself.

UNIT VIII: UNDERSTANDING AND IMPROVING YOUR MEMORY

When asked what problems they experience in learning, a high percentage of college students report difficulties with remembering. Educators have known a good deal about the ways in which human memory works for at least several decades, yet we have not effectively conveyed this understanding to our students. The vast majority of students graduate from high school and, in many cases, college without experiencing any instruction in the workings of memory.

This unit seeks to introduce students in a clear and simple way to several basic concepts involving the nature and function of memory. These include short and long term memory, specific skills which aid memory, mnemonics, and the relationship between memory and learning style. The unit's activities engage students in the initial use of a number of memory skills which offer both immediate and long-range value.

Of course, this unit is only a beginning which you may wish to expand or amplify.

If you are not familiar with the relationship between visualization and memory as discussed in this unit, you may want to examine *Seeing With The Mind's Eye* by Mike and Nancy Samuels (New York: Random House, 1975).

Suggested Directions for Unit VIII

1. Ask your students to read "An Experiment With Memory" (page 73) and do the experiment. When they are done, collect the results by a show of hands ("How many people have one right from List A? Two? Three? . . ."), and plot the results on two graphs on the board. Most of your students will probably have more correct from List B than from List A. Ask them to reflect on this result and offer explanations for it. Discuss why it is easier to remember information when it is logically organized than when it is random.

   Approximate time: 10–15 minutes

2. Have your students read "How Does Memory Work?" (page 74) and "From Short Term To Long Term" (page 74). Discuss for emphasis. Ask students to offer other examples of rote memory and logical memory.

   Approximate time: 5–10 minutes

3. Ask students to read "The Keys To Remembering" (pages 74–75). If useful, go over each of the four keys, and ask students to offer examples.

   Approximate time: 8 minutes

4. Have students read "Applying The Keys To Remembering" (page 75) and "The Cause/ Effect Pattern" (page 75). Discuss as is useful.

   Approximate time: 5 minutes

5. Ask students to do Practice 1 (pages 76–77). When they are done, ask them to form small groups of three members (if necessary, some groups can be two or four), and share their answers to the practice with other group members. If useful or necessary, you may want to go over the answers briefly with the whole class.

Approximate time: 15–20 minutes

6. Ask your students to read the instructions for Practice 2 (page 77). Allow them four minutes to study, and then give the quiz below, or one of your own writing which may be more appropriate. Then, briefly go over the quiz.

PRACTICE QUIZ

1. What is the main reason why students work after school?	INFLATION
2–4. What are three effects on students' school lives of part-time jobs? (any three)	NO VARSITY SPORTS, LESS HOMEWORK DONE, ACADEMIC DEFICIENCIES, PHYSICAL AND MENTAL FATIGUE, ABSENCE, TEACHERS BECOME REMEDIATORS
5. What does Manning suggest as a cure?	A CHANGE IN VALUES AWAY FROM MATERIALISM AND TOWARDS EDUCATION

Approximate time: 10–12 minutes

7. Have your students do Practice 3 (page 78) and share their responses and experience with their group. You may wish to have a whole class discussion at the end of this sharing as a way of emphasizing the students' learnings and insights.

Approximate time: 5–10 minutes

8. Have your students read "The Comparison/Contrast Pattern" (page 78), and do Practices 4 and 5 (pages 78–79). When they are done, have students share their charts with their group members.

Approximate time: 15–25 minutes

9. Have students read the instructions for Practice 6 (page 79). Allow them four minutes to study. Then, give them the quiz below, or a quiz which you write. Go over the quiz. Then, discuss what your students have learned by practicing the "four keys" a second time.

PRACTICE QUIZ: True or False

T   1. Hersey had privileged access to both Truman and Ford.

F   2. Hersey could attend all of Ford's daily meetings.

T   3. Both Ford and Truman were relatively lack-luster presidents.

F   4. Times were good when both Ford and Truman entered office.

F   5. Both men were elected to office.

T   6. Truman knew his history well.

F   7. Truman was highly secretive.

F   8. Ford reached office through the death of his predecessor.

Approximate time: 10-12 minutes

10. Ask your students to read "More Hints For Improving Memory" (page 80). Go over and discuss the examples.

Approximate time: 8 minutes

ANSWERS FOR PRACTICES IN UNIT VIII

Page 77: Practice 1

1. Saps buying power
2. Skews learning habits
3. Subverts values

Inflation causes students to get **part-time jobs.**
        Part-time jobs cause students not to take part in
        varsity sports and do less **homework.**
                Doing less **homework** causes students
                to become deficient in **basic academic skills.**
                        This deficiency in students causes
                        teachers **to become remediators.**
                Part-time jobs also cause students to
                experience **physical and mental fatigue.**
        This causes frequent **absences.**
Primary motive for part-time work: **indulgent self interest**

Manning's suggested cure: **change in values towards education, away from materialism**

Pages 78-79: Practice 4

both	in contrast	differences
different	pairing	
dissimilar	similarities	

Page 79: Practice 5

POINTS OF COMPARISON/ CONTRAST	Truman	Ford
Access Hersey had	Privileged, total freedom	Privileged, but not to meetings with Kissinger
Personality	Feisty, confident, lack-luster	Cheerful, pleasant, cautious, secretive, passive, lack-luster
Background and ability	Intelligent, well versed in history, well counseled by able people	Little understanding of history, acceding to advisors
Method of entering office	Succeeded after death of predecessor, not elected	Succeeded after scandal, not elected
Conditions in country when term began	Tough times	Tough times

More Hints: Page 80

1a. If a "c" you do spy,
     Place the "e" before the "i."
     If you do not spy a "c,"
     Place the "i" before the "e."

 b. FBI = Federal Bureau of Investigation
     NATO = North Atlantic Treaty Organization
     SNAFU = situation normal, all fouled up

 c. green = genus
     stamps = species

54

EXTENSION ACTIVITIES

1. Have blank tapes, tape recorders, and several passages of reading material available. Let students study from a summary, outline, or map they have made after reading one of the passages. Have them recall the ideas on paper without looking back. Then, have the same students read a similar passage, tape a summary of it, and study by listening to the tape. Again, have them recall the ideas on paper without looking back. Then, ask them to compare the results of seeing versus listening as a way of study.

   If students learn well by listening, encourage them to purchase an inexpensive tape recorder for study. If they cannot afford a tape recorder, suggest that they study by reading their notes aloud where they won't bother anybody. Or have two students who learn best by listening study together. One can read while the other listens, and then they can reverse the process.

2. To improve students' ability to visualize, have them read or listen to material that is high in visual content. Ask them to take notes using a visual device(s) such as a stick drawing, a simple picture, or a diagram.

3. Have students look through their textbooks for important ideas and concepts that can be illustrated. Let both the artists and the non-artists share their illustrations on the chalkboard or on paper.

4. Ask students to develop their own motivational questions, the "be interested" step of the keys to remembering. They can do this by surveying a textbook chapter or section and writing a "problem" that could be answered by reading the chapter or section.

   EXAMPLE OF A "PROBLEM" (for a section on the Westernization of Russia):

   > You are a member of the landlord class living in Russia in the years after 1682. How is your life changing politically, economically, and socially from what it was before 1682?

5. Give students a list of facts to memorize. Ask them to *elaborate* on those facts by thinking about what they already know about them, using their *imaginations* to express the facts as images, and drawing *inferences* about the facts. Forming *interconnections* and increasing the *context* for the facts enhances memory.

6. The *method of loci* helps when certain items must be memorized. Give students a list of items and ask them to link each item with a fixed path. The path can be through the woods, through a house, through a building, etc. For example, relate item 1 to the front door, item 2 to the hallway, item 3 to the stairs, etc. This silly method works because it imposes *organization* on an otherwise random list and because it makes the mind *process deeper* and *form connections*.

7. Similar to the method of loci is the *peg word* method of remembering. Give students a list of items and ask them to link each item with one in a jingle. Any jingle such as this will do:

One is a bun.	Six is sticks.
Two is a shoe.	Seven is heaven.
Three is a tree.	Eight is a gate.
Four is a door.	Nine is a line.
Five is a hive.	Ten is a hen.

First, students memorize the jingle (it can be used over and over again for different memory tasks). Then, they relate the first item to be memorized to the bun, the second to the shoe, etc. Again, *elaboration, interconnections,* and *deeper processing* are the keys to memorizing.

UNIT VIII SUMMARY: UNDERSTANDING AND IMPROVING YOUR MEMORY

Human memory works on two different levels:

Short term memory includes what you focus on in the moment, what holds your attention. Most people can only hold about 7 pieces of information in short term memory.

To retain and recall information, you must transfer it into *long term memory* which includes all the information you know and can remember.

Two ways of moving information into long term memory are *rote learning* and *learning through understanding.*

Rote learning means learning through repetition.

Learning through understanding involves learning and remembering by understanding the relationships among ideas and information.

Four keys to remembering are:

1. Choose to remember   Be interested. Pay attention. Want to learn and remember. Consciously choose to remember.

2. Visualize   Visualize or picture in your mind what you wish to remember.

3. Relate   Relate ideas and information you wish to remember to each other and to ideas and information you already know.

4. Repeat   Even though you've already learned something, go over it one more time so you can overlearn it. Be sure to say it in your own words.

Becoming aware of the pattern of organization used in an article or lecture can also help you to learn and remember. Two commonly used patterns are (1) cause/effect and (2) comparison/contrast.

Other ways to improve your memory include:

1. Using mnemonic (memory aiding) devices such as rhymes, acronyms, and silly sentences.

2. Using your learning style strengths.

3. Summarizing lectures and articles, and going over your summaries right after you write them.

UNIT IX: READING FLEXIBLY

Many research studies have demonstrated that one of the most important characteristics of excellent readers is their ability to change their reading rate depending on (1) the kind of material being read; (2) the purpose for reading; and (3) the difficulty of reading material in terms of their own background. The ability to change reading rate in light of these factors is called *reading flexibility.*

Poor and average readers tend to read everything from "Dear Abby" to a physics text at the same rate. They begin with the title and plod through every word until they reach the end. In contrast, excellent readers quickly survey their task first and choose an appropriate rate of reading. Depending on the material and their purpose, they may read only for main ideas and skim over or omit examples, details, and even whole sections if they find them irrelevant to their goals. Or, they may read slowly with painstaking care.

The purpose of this unit is to introduce students to the idea of reading flexibly, that is, changing their reading rate to meet their needs. The unit is also designed to involve students in some initial practice of the skills involved in flexible reading.

> *Please Note:* For *Practice 4* on page 85, students will need to use one of their own textbooks. Be sure to ask them to bring a textbook to class on the day when you work on this practice.

READING FLEXIBILITY — CHANGE AND GUILT

Some students may ask: "Why shouldn't I read slowly and carefully? I've always done my reading that way, and my grades are good."

You may want to respond to this by noting that many students do well, particularly in high school, in spite of their slow reading rate, not because of it. You may also want to sketch out the much heavier reading load which students face in college compared to that in high school.

Another kind of response involves stressing the ways in which flexible reading is more efficient than one slow reading rate. Some of these are:

1. Flexible reading is more efficient. You can accomplish more in the same amount of time.

2. Flexible reading aids comprehension. Slow readers do not comprehend as well as readers of similar ability who vary their rate. Slow readers can't interrelate information as well as flexible readers.

3. Flexible reading is directed. You focus your effort on what's important.

4. Flexible reading aids memory. When you think about what's important in a reading and set a framework for it, you're much more likely to retain it.

5. Flexible reading is the most feasible way to complete college reading assignments successfully.

It's natural for students to feel committed to habits which they believe helped them to succeed in the past. The most respectful and effective way to teach flexible reading is to explain what the skills are and why they work, give students an opportunity to try them, and help students discover the benefits of flexible reading through their analysis of their own experience.

A final word: some students feel guilty if they don't read every word in an assignment. You may want to address this concern by discussing it in terms of the student's purpose for reading. Focus on the idea that you read for a purpose. Often you don't need to read every word, every section, or even every assignment to achieve your purpose. And there's nothing wrong with omitting that which you know you don't need. You might also want to share some of your own experience of learning to become a flexible reader.

FLEXIBLE READING AND SPEED READING

Flexible reading is *not* speed reading, although speed reading may be one rate which a reader uses. It's important to note that this unit does not teach speed reading.

The value of speed reading is discussed in the "Learning Study Skills On Your Own" section at the end of the unit. Speed reading is a relatively simple and immensely valuable skill which, for some reason, schools have almost totally ignored. We urge you to examine this skill carefully in the source cited in "Learning Study Skills On Your Own" and elsewhere. You may want to develop your own speed reading skills and then help your students develop theirs.

USING AN ENCYCLOPEDIA

Although some college instructors will not permit the use of an encyclopedia as a source, an encyclopedia entry is still a good starting point for a student who is tackling an unfamiliar subject. In view of this value (and aware of possible protests), we have included an entry from an encyclopedia as a resource in this unit.

Suggested Directions for Unit IX

1. Have your students read "What Is Flexible Reading?" (page 82). Discuss the three factors which affect rate. Have several students share their own examples for each factor.

   Approximate time: 3–5 minutes

2. Have your students complete Practice 1 (page 82). Tell them that they will come back to it in a few minutes. Then, ask them to read "Different Rates Of Reading" (pages 82–83). Discuss each of the four rates. Have students give examples of when they use each.

   Approximate time: 7 minutes

3. Have your students do Practice 2 (page 83). Discuss the ways in which reading rates do (or should) vary for different kinds of reading. Ask students to give examples from their responses to Practices 1 and 2.

   Approximate time: 5 minutes

4. Ask your students to read "Using Different Reading Rates" (page 83) and do Practice 3 (pages 83–84). When they are done, have them form pairs, and ask them to share their questions, answers, and other notes with each other. Then, discuss the different rates of reading they used with the whole class.

    Approximate time: 15–20 minutes

5. Have your students read "Using Your Rapid Reading Rate" (page 85) and the directions for Practice 4 (page 85). Discuss as is useful. Tell students that you will announce the timing. (Some students may complain about the brevity of time allowed. Encourage them just to try it out and see what happens.) Give them 3 minutes to survey, then 8 minutes to read rapidly. Ask your students to discuss their experience with their partners for a few minutes. Then, engage them in a whole class discussion about the usefulness of rapid reading. Ask several students to share their estimations.

    Approximate time: 20 minutes

6. Give students the choice of working on the rest of the unit individually or in pairs. When they have decided, have them read "Flexible Reading For Research" (page 85). Discuss as is needed. Then, ask students to do Practice 5 (pages 85–86) and Practice 6 (page 86). When they are done, go over the practices.

    Approximate time: 10–15 minutes

7. Have your students do Practice 7 (pages 86–88). Go over their responses to the questions and the various sections of the article which they marked. (You may want to do this with the whole class or in small groups.) Then, have students discuss their experience of reading flexibly.

    Approximate time: 20 minutes

8. Follow the same procedure for Practice 8 (pages 88–89) as you did for Practice 7.

    Approximate time: 15–20 minutes

ANSWERS FOR PRACTICES IN UNIT IX

Pages 82–83: Practices 1–2

Answers will vary.

Pages 83–84: Practice 3

Questions, answers, and notes will vary. Questions should include some of the following:

What is the "third world"?	"Have-not" countries, mostly undeveloped, whose interests are different from the "free" and Communist "worlds."
Does the "third world" have clout in global affairs?	Yes, based on control of natural resources and large numbers in the UN General Assembly and other bodies.
Are all "third world" nations poor?	No. Another determination of inclusion is a feeling of having been cheated by lighter-skinned, "northern" nations. Most of the "third world" countries are "southern," have darker-skinned populations.

| Who are the targets of the "third world"? | USA, Western European nations, Soviet Union. |
| Does the talk of different worlds really mean something? | Yes. It has both moral and economic aspects to it, and it's very real. |

Page 86: Practice 5

Arlex, Bertrand, Jackson, Richards

Check "Richards" twice as it is directly relevant and most current.

Page 86: Practice 6

Applications: medicine	Dental drilling
Applied laser principles	Fiber-optic scalpel
Bloodless surgery	Surgery

If students can support other answers than those above, accept them.

Pages 86–88: Practice 7

Answers will vary. Accept any answers which students can support. Suggested answers are as follows:

Checks next to: paragraphs 1, 2, 3 and possibly 4 in the first section
the paragraph "In Medicine"
paragraphs 1–4 in "How a Laser Works"

X next to: will vary; ask students to explain their choices

1. The rest of the article would not be helpful, unless the student wants to include material about the history of lasers in the paper's introduction.

2. Answers will vary. Ask students to explain their choices.

Pages 88–89: Practice 8

Answers will vary. Accept any answers which students can support. Suggested answers are:

Checks next to: paragraphs in the "Medicine" section

1–3. Answers will vary.

EXTENSION ACTIVITIES

1. Have students establish their "four" reading rates. Time them on materials that call for all four rates. Be sure to check comprehension in some way. Encourage students to practice the four rates for two or three weeks, and time them again for comparison.

    You may want to have students record their results on a chart like the one below.

STUDENT DIRECTIONS AND CHART:

For a few weeks, fill in the chart to analyze your reading flexibility. Beside each rate note the book or magazine you use. (Don't use more than one book or magazine for each rate, or you won't be comparing similar things.) Write the amount of time you practice each rate each day or so. Then, write the number of pages read (use fractions if necessary) and under it a " + " for good comprehension or a " − " for poor comprehension.

RATES	BOOK OR JOURNAL	TIME	PAGES READ/COMPREHENSION
SKIM			
RAPID			
AVERAGE			
SLOW			

2. Encourage students to read chapters of a textbook or other non-fiction book as they did in Practice 4. Ask them to aim at completing the survey/rapid reading of a chapter in 30 minutes or less. Later they can read in more detail and take notes, if necessary.

3. Teach the *paper clip technique*. Have students read a fairly easy book for 10 minutes and mark where they end. Next, they count the pages they read. Then, they take a paperclip and attach it one page beyond the number of pages they just read. Allow 10 minutes to reach the clip. Each time they read, have them add one or one-half page to be read in the same amount of time.

Be sure to allow recall time after each reading.

UNIT IX SUMMARY: READING FLEXIBLY

Flexible reading means learning to vary your reading rate according to:

1. The kind of material you are reading

2. The purpose for which you are reading

3. The difficulty of the reading material for you

Think of flexible reading as shifting into different gears depending on what you are reading and for what purpose.

Four different reading rates are:

1. Skimming and scanning rate	Reading only key words, phrases, and sentences. Or, quickly searching for particular information. A very fast rate useful for surveying and finding specific information.
2. Rapid reading rate	Pushing your normal reading rate faster on purpose. Useful when you are reading only for main ideas or for review.
3. Average reading rate	The rate at which you ordinarily read material of average difficulty. Useful when you want to know details as well as main ideas.
4. Slow reading rate	Reading more slowly and deliberately than your average reading rate. Useful for difficult and/or technical reading.

For actual reading, you'll want to use several or all four rates while you read a chapter or article. The skilled reader changes gears often.

Reading flexibly can help you do research for research papers more effectively and efficiently. For example, you can skim or scan the entries in a card catalogue to find ones which are relevant for your topic. Once you locate useful books, you can skim their indexes to help you locate passages in the books which are directly related to your topic.

When you read any sources, for example, journal articles or articles in encyclopedias or elsewhere, you can use skimming, rapid reading, average reading, and slow reading as these rates are helpful to you.

UNIT X: GAINING FROM DISCUSSIONS

Instructors use discussions to promote both independent and interdependent learning. For example, a discussion about a group of articles requires that a student first have read and reacted to the ideas in those articles independently. Then, students and instructor contribute, question, and evaluate ideas and views in class. A good discussion generates student-student and student-instructor interdependence in learning.

Another value of discussions is the wider range of ideas and opinions which can be generated when people from varied backgrounds contribute. The more voices heard, the greater the potential for the expression of divergent thinking.

Discussions can also help students to see course material as more relevant, because they relate ideas discussed to their own lives. Both this relevance and the activity of discussions can engage students' interests and motivations in a powerful way.

Finally, discussions can engage students in three important aspects of learning: (1) thinking in the ways of a subject, i.e., thinking like a scientist or an historian; (2) speaking the vocabulary of the subject; and (3) listening to ideas about the subject and reacting to them.

The purpose of this unit is to deepen your students' understanding of the nature of class discussions and their potential value for learning. The practice is designed to help your students become more aware of their current behavior in discussions and to suggest ways in which they can change to gain more from this kind of class.

Please Note: This unit will require 2-3 class periods.

Suggested Directions for Unit X

DAY ONE

1. Ask your students to read "Why Have Class Discussions?" (page 92). Discuss for emphasis. You may want to share with students some of your own values or experiences which relate to this section.

   Approximate time: 3-5 minutes

2. Ask each student to find a partner. Then, have your students read "What Makes A Good Discussion?" (page 92), think about the questions, talk them over with their partner, and then answer them. When they are done (you may wish to set a time limit), have a number of students share their lists orally. Write the characteristics cited on the board. Keep going until you have lists which include all of your students' suggestions. Then, ask your students to analyze the two lists of characteristics and discuss them.

   Approximate time: 10 minutes

3. Have your students read "The Basics of Discussions" (page 92). Discuss for emphasis.

   Approximate time: 3 minutes

4. Have your students read the directions for Practice 1 (page 93). Organize your class into groups of 6–8 members. Then, go over the directions orally in this way:

Go over the *recorder's* role. Then, ask one student in each group to volunteer to act as recorder. Give the recorders an opportunity to ask questions about their job.

Go over the *observer's* role in general. Ask one student from each group to volunteer to act as observer. Once this is done, have all of your students read the "Observer's Form" on page 94. Go over each role, clarifying and giving examples or asking students to give examples. Tell the observers that it's possible for a speaker to fulfill more than one role at a time. For examples, someone might *summarize* and then *add* information in the same comment. You may also wish to give the observers a model for scoring like the one below.

ROLES	Sue	Bill
1. ENCOURAGING ...	ⅧⅡ 7	ⅠⅠⅡⅠ 4

Give the observers a chance to ask questions about their job.

Remind your class that those who are not observers or recorders will be participants. Ask your students to examine the "Participant's Form" on page 93. Explain and clarify as needed.

Approximate time: 20 minutes

DAY TWO

5. Briefly review the discussion roles. Then, present your students with a *problem* for discussion which is appropriate for your course. Try to select a problem which is interesting and involving. (Or, you may choose to use the problem described below.) Give your students 15 minutes for discussion, and then call a halt. Allow about 5 minutes for the observers and participants to complete their forms. Ask your students to read "Sharing The Results" (page 95) and "Making Sense Of The Results" (page 95) when they have completed their forms.

Approximate time: 30 minutes

* * * * * * * * * * * * * *

PROBLEM FOR DISCUSSION

Your school or college has gained access to a graphic computer terminal for four hours each weekday afternoon from one to five. An operator will be available during those hours, and the room housing the computer terminal will be open to you.

Decide how your school or college should use the available computer time.

If you use this problem: (1) have your students re-read the article about computer graphics on pages 55–56 for homework the night before the class discussion;

(2) you may want to give your students a few starting questions, e.g., What courses could use computer graphics? What might the administration do with this type of computer?

* * * * * * * * * * * * * *

6. When students are ready, have them share their evaluations as indicated in "Sharing The Results." You may want to move among the groups and listen and contribute as you see fit.

Approximate time: 10–15 minutes

7. You may want to have a short, whole class discussion when the small groups are done. This discussion can give students an opportunity to share what they've learned with their peers and to raise any questions. (You may need some time in a third class to accomplish this.)

Approximate time: 5–10 minutes

8. Finally, ask your students to read "Preparing For Discussions" (page 95) and the Unit Summary (page 96).

Approximate time: 3 minutes

EXTENSION ACTIVITIES

1. Ask students (working in groups, if you wish) to make up a rating sheet to rate you, the instructor, as you lead class discussions. Then, conduct a discussion with the class and have each student rate you. Discuss results with the class.

2. Videotape or tape-record students' first efforts at guided discussion. Do the same for a later discussion. Play back each immediately following the respective discussions, and then play back both tapes on the same day so students can discuss their progress. Taping is threatening at first to students, but they soon learn to enjoy it if the discussions following the taping sessions are conducted in a spirit of charity, fun, and learning.

3. Allow students time to rate a regular class discussion using the participant and observer forms. When you copy the observer form after the first discussion, don't bother to copy the definitions of each role. Students may refer to their books.

4. To link discussions with writing, ask each group of discussants to present its arguments in written form as a report after the discussion.

5. Over a two week period, have students collect information on a topic(s) of interest. Share the materials within the class, having students take any notes they wish. Then, discuss the topic(s) in small groups using rating sheets like those in the student book.

6. Have students work in groups, each group responsible for a particular day's class discussion. The group can assign prereading questions and will be responsible for conducting a lively discussion during all or part of a class period.

7. Encourage students working in discussion groups to do divergent or elaborative thinking. Set up questions on class materials, or have students do it using their knowledge of exploratory questions. Then, ask them to brainstorm for answers.

UNIT X SUMMARY: GAINING FROM DISCUSSIONS

Class discussions give students an opportunity to express, explore, test, and share ideas, understandings, opinions, and questions. *Good* discussions can help you learn, and they can be enjoyable.

Good discussions require:

1. Participants who discuss actively, listen well, and contribute a fair share without dominating or withdrawing
2. A topic for discussion, and ideas, information, theories, feelings, and questions relating to that topic

Ways in which people contribute to the effectiveness of a discussion include:

participating actively

listening carefully and actively

encouraging others

questioning

adding information, ideas, and opinions

clarifying

summarizing

compromising and peacemaking

When you can, try to be prepared for class discussions, so that you'll have more to contribute and more to gain.

UNIT XI: LEARNING FROM VISUALS

This unit is designed to help students become more aware of the many ways in which they can learn from visuals and to engage them in developing specific skills for this purpose. The unit also is intended to aid students in the improvement of their ability to ask useful questions in relation to visuals and text.

The unit does not attempt to work with every kind of visual but to introduce methods which can be applied to any kind of picture, image, or representation.

Skilled learners question as they read and listen. They relate new information to old and consider the value and legitimacy of what they are hearing or reading. For them, reading and listening are a lot like having a conversation. The questioning strategies introduced in this unit can be applied by students to visuals, texts, and lectures. And their use can help students to become more effective learners.

Suggested Directions for Unit XI

1. Ask your students to read "What Is A Picture Worth?" (page 97) and respond to the question. When your students are ready, have several people share their responses with the class. Discuss, underlining the capacity of visuals to convey meaning.

    Approximate time: 10 minutes

2. Have your students read "The Value Of Visuals" (page 98). Discuss as is useful. Then, have them read "Time Line" (page 98) and do Practice 1 (page 98). Have students share their time lines with a partner, or have a few students show their time lines to whole class.

    Approximate time: 10 minutes

3. Ask your students to read "Graph" (page 99) and complete Practice 2 (page 99). Have students share their graphs and conclusions with a partner(s). Discuss with the whole class as is useful.

    Approximate time: 10–15 minutes

4. Have your students read "Asking Exploratory Questions" (page 100) and do Practice 3 (page 100). Ask several or many students to read their questions aloud. Ask students if they can categorize the questions read into any patterns.

    Approximate time: 10 minutes

5. Ask your students to read "Using Visual And Text Together" (page 100) and do Practice 4 (page 101). Have students share their questions with a partner(s) or with the whole class. Again, discuss any patterns they see in the kinds of questions.

    Approximate time: 7 minutes

6. Have students read "Asking Questions About Visuals And Text" (page 101). Discuss briefly for emphasis. Then, ask students to do Practice 5 (pages 102-103). When students are ready, go over the practice. Elicit several responses to each item.

   Approximate time: 15 minutes

7. Ask students to do Practice 6 (pages 104-106). Have them share their notes and questions with a partner(s). Ask them to discuss their questions.

   Approximate time: 20 minutes

8. Ask your students to read "Visuals And Learning Style" (page 107). Discuss as is useful.

   Approximate time: 5 minutes

ANSWERS FOR PRACTICES IN UNIT XI

Page 98: Practice 1

Title: *American Involvement in Wars in the 20th Century*

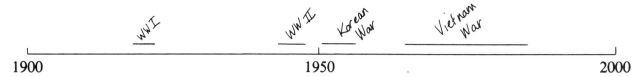

Page 99: Practice 2

Answers will vary depending on how students choose to structure the graph. The conclusion involves the vast increase in cotton imports and, by inference, a corresponding growth in the industry which used raw cotton to produce cloth and other goods.

Page 100: Practice 3

Answers will vary. Be sure that questions are exploratory, that is, that they go beyond the literal and involve creative, critical, and inferential processes.

Page 101: Practice 4

Questions will vary.

Pages 102-103: Practice 5

Questions will vary. Note that the event pictured is related to the Boston Tea Party. The tarred and feathered tax collector is being forced to drink tea by citizens of Boston. A noose hangs from the "liberty tree," and a handbill about the Stamp Act is posted upside down on the tree. In the background, men are throwing tea off the ship into the harbor.

Pages 104–106: Practice 6

Example of notes:

> Theory of the Tigris/Euphrates valleys as cradle of civilization (7–8,000 years ago) under attack:
>
> 1. East Africa — humans herded cattle 15,000 yrs ago
>
> 2. Nile valley — humans grew barley 18,000 yrs ago
>
> 3. S. Eurasia — humans domesticated cattle 8,000 yrs ago
>
> 4. SE Asia — humans cultivated plants 12–7,000 yrs ago

Questions will vary.

EXTENSION ACTIVITIES

1. Using a literary book with some pictures, have students view the pictures first, read the story, and compare: Is the artist's rendition accurate and true? Biased? Did the artist choose the most important events to picture? Why did the artist picture this event and not another? Explain all answers.

2. Use visuals to compare and contrast:

    > e.g., air view vs. ground view
    > city or town today with city or town years ago
    > one artist's conception of the theme with another artist's

3. Use visuals to clarify:

    > e.g., concept in history — early Egypt, modern Africa
    > meaning of words — esker, dome

    Have students make a picture dictionary for books without pictures; duplicate it and give it to the class.

4. Use visuals to aid recall and review. Have students look at a set of pictures and explain concepts learned that are illustrated by the pictures.

5. Use visuals to motivate, initiate, create an atmosphere. Have students look at a set of pictures before studying a segment of work. Talk about what they know of the items pictured.

6. Use visuals to indicate a sequence of events or a process. Or, have students fill in missing parts of a visual sequence.

7. Use visuals to aid higher level thinking:

    a. Have students view biased or propagandistic visuals and discuss or write about them.

    b. Have students view visuals that enhance insight and appreciation of a work of literature, art, etc.

    c. Have students discuss concepts, ideas, and problems as they look at visuals. They may ask questions like "What is the solution to the problem in this picture?" "What effects will this event have?" etc.

8. Read a description or a set of directions aloud and have students draw it after you finish.

UNIT XI SUMMARY: LEARNING FROM VISUALS

Visuals such as pictures, charts, maps, graphs, and cartoons are very effective at communicating concepts, relationships, and details. In a text or article, each visual usually conveys one main idea which complements what is expressed in writing.

You can use visuals to provoke exploratory questions. When you look carefully at a visual, it often prompts questions of this sort in you. And when you answer the exploratory questions, you can learn a great deal.

Interesting and helpful exploratory questions often relate to (1) *patterns of organization,* such as cause/effect, list, definition, sequence/time, description/narration, and comparison/contrast, (2) *evaluation,* and (3) *appreciation.*

In a book or article, the text and visuals are designed to complement each other so that each helps to explain, clarify, and develop the other.

Even if you are not an artist, you can still use visuals to help you learn. And the more that you use them, the more helpful they will become to you.

UNIT XII: PREPARING FOR AND TAKING EXAMS

In high school many students never go beyond a few hours of hasty, "last minute" review as a way of studying for exams. Academic success in college requires greater skill and effort in exam preparation.

This unit presents your students with the idea that organized study for an exam is much more helpful than any kind of general review. It offers students a clear strategy for exam preparation and initial practice in the use of this strategy. Finally the unit introduces the concept of "testwiseness" along with activities which help students become more "testwise."

Please Note: The practices in much of this unit essentially constitute a *simulation.* Students are introduced to a five step strategy and are asked to practice each step in relation to a course they are actually taking. To complete these activities, students need their course materials (books, notes, etc.) at hand.

On the day before you begin this unit, explain its format to your students. Ask them to select a course with which to work and to bring the necessary materials with them to class for the next meeting.

Organize students to work in pairs or trios with others who are taking the same course.

(If you are teaching this unit at the end of a semester, you may want to change its status from that of a simulation to an actual preparation for an impending exam. Introducing this element of realism can help students to see the value of strategic study even more powerfully.)

This is a long unit. You may want to assign sections of it for homework.

Suggested Directions for Unit XII

1. Have students who are working together sit next to each other.

2. Have your students read the "Introduction" (page 109), "Long-Term Preparation" (page 109), and "A Study Strategy For Exams" (page 109). Discuss as is useful. Then, have your students read "I. Survey Your Study Problem" (page 109). Discuss briefly. Explain that part of this involves "psyching out" the instructor and the exam, that is, figuring out as best you can what the exam will include.

   Approximate time: 10 minutes

3. Ask your students to do Practice 1 (page 110) individually and then compare their responses with those of their partner(s). Discuss as is useful. Have several students share their responses to part C.

   Approximate time: 10 minutes

4. Have your students read "II. Organize Your Information" (page 111) and do Practice 2 (page 112) individually. Then, have students share outlines or maps with their partners. With the whole class, discuss the value of question maps or outlines. Also, note that long range planners create a file of 3 x 5 cards listing important terms, rules, and facts as they encounter them during the semester and then can use these cards for study.

   Approximate time: 20 minutes

5. Ask your students to read "III. Work With Your Information And Learn It" (page 1i3), and complete Practice 3 (page 114). Discuss the students' evaluations of the various suggestions.

   Approximate time: 15 minutes

6. Ask your students to read "IV. Take The Exam" (pages 114–115), and do Practice 4 (page 115). Discuss as is useful with the whole group, or have each small group discuss the suggestions selected.

   Approximate time: 10–15 minutes

7. Have your students read "Learn From The Results" (page 115). Discuss as is useful.

   Approximate time: 5 minutes

8. Ask your students to read "Common Types Of Exam Questions" (page 115) and "Short Answer Questions" (page 115). Then, have them complete Practice 5 (page 116).

   Approximate time: 10 minutes

9. Have your students read "Essay Questions" (page 116). Discuss as is useful. Then, have your students read steps #1 and #2 (page 117) and do Practice 6 (page 117). When students are ready, discuss the definitions, polish them, and have students write them into their "glossary."

   Approximate time: 15–20 minutes

10. Ask students to do Practice 7 (page 117) individually and share their questions with their partner(s). Or, have several students share their questions with the whole class. Discuss as is useful.

    Approximate time: 5–8 minutes

11. Have students read step #3 (page 118) and do Practice 8 (page 118). Then, have students read step #4 (page 118) and complete Practice 9 (pages 118-119). Set a 5 minute time limit for Practice 9. Then, have students share their notes with their partners.

    Approximate time: 15 minutes

12. Have students read steps #5 and #6 (pages 119-120). Discuss as is useful.

    Approximate time: 5 minutes

13. Ask your students to read "Multiple Choice Questions" (page 120) and do Practice 10 (page 120). Discuss as is useful.

    Approximate time: 10 minutes

14. Have your students read "Problems" (page 121) and "A Final Word: 'Testwiseness'" (page 121). Discuss "testwiseness" and emphasize its importance.

    Approximate time: 7 minutes

ANSWERS FOR PRACTICES IN UNIT XII

All answers in this unit will vary according to students' choices except for Practice 6 (page 117).

These definitions are suggested. Accept any reasonable response.

   analyze: break the subject down into its essential parts and critically analyze those parts

   compare: show similarities and differences between things

   contrast: show differences between things

   describe: give the features of something in detail

   discuss: tell what you know about a subject, trying to give a balanced presentation

   evaluate/criticize: judge a subject carefully, giving positive and negative aspects

   explain: clarify and interpret the details of a subject

   outline: organize the main ideas and supporting details of a subject in a way which shows relationships

   summarize: give a brief account of the main features of a subject

   trace (or "trace the development of"): follow the development of a subject step by step in sequence or in chronological order

EXTENSION ACTIVITIES

1. Have students, working in small groups, prepare an exam study guide according to patterns of organization. Each group, using the materials of the course — reading and lecture notes, lists of course objectives, etc. — will generate exam questions according to category. Have students enter the type of question at the top of a page, write the question on the left, and fill in a brief answer on the right. (Answers may be mapped, outlined, or in summary form, etc.) See the example below.

DEFINITIONS

monarchy	gov't ruled by absolute ruler, e.g., king
oligarchy	gov't ruled by a few or by a faction

See a list of question types in the student book.

If possible, duplicate copies of all questions and answers for each class member, and choose some or all of your exam from student questions.

2. Have students generate essay questions and answers based on a chapter in their textbook. Assign or allow students to choose from the types of questions they listed and defined in their student books. If several students use the same textbook, let them swap questions and write answers. Students taking the "test" should compare with an answer key prepared by the student designing the test. Be sure to spot-check answers yourself.

3. Many tests make use of verbal analogies. Help students to deal with this type of test by keeping on hand sets of verbal analogies from exam preparation and vocabulary books. Teach students to analyze the *kind of relationship* in the analogy. Allow them to work in pairs and use reference books as they analyze and answer.

Here are some common kinds of relationships found in analogies:

RELATIONSHIP	EXAMPLE
part/whole	wheel/car
word/antonym	top/bottom
object/use	scissors/cut
raw material/product	pine tree/turpentine
adult/child	dog/puppy
etc.	

There are many other types of relationships which students can analyze and understand.

4. To enhance students' problem solving ability and thinking in general, collect problems from your content area or from several content areas. Have students work on the problems in small groups or with a partner. When a student thinks he or she has an answer, that student must explain the whole solution orally including the steps used in solving the problem.

5. Using a set of math problems, have students try to estimate answers within a limited time period. Let the best estimators lead the discussion on how to estimate in a given situation. Estimation is very important, especially in multiple choice exams.

6. Many students like to organize their test review on tape, especially if they are auditory learners. One way to teach this is to have students record a review question, say "stop," then read the answer on tape. When students study from the tape, they stop the recorder at the word "stop," recite the answer and listen to see if they are correct.

UNIT XII: SUMMARY: PREPARING FOR AND TAKING EXAMS

When you study for exams, use a strategy like the one below.

1. **Survey your study problem**

   Ask yourself and then answer the following questions:

   A. What do I need to know for this exam?

   B. Of what I think is likely to be on the exam, what do I already know?

   C. Of what is likely to be on the exam, what don't I already know?

   D. How much time do I have to study?

2. **Organize your information**

   Decide what the most important information is from your notes, books, etc., and organize it to make it easier to work with and learn. Write important terms, rules, and facts on 3 x 5 cards. Diagram, map, chart, or graph information so you can easily see relationships. Create a *question outline* or *question map* to help you organize your studying.

3. **Work with your information and learn it**

   Use your question outline or map by asking yourself the questions and rehearsing your answers. Study your maps, graphs, charts, diagrams, and 3 x 5 cards. Reinforce your memory by restating information in different words, explaining ideas and concepts to someone else, evaluating and criticizing material, and using mental images or drawing pictures to illustrate important concepts. Practice any skills that you'll need to use on the exam. Finally, think about what kinds of test questions you expect to encounter on the exam, and prepare for them in any way that you can.

4. **Take the exam**

   Be physically prepared. When you receive the exam, survey it, and plan your timing for answering the questions. Read the directions carefully. Give the most direct answer you can. Be sure to answer all questions, unless there's a penalty for guessing. While you take the exam, keep yourself focused on what you need to do. Don't let yourself be distracted by others.

5. **Learn from the results**

   When you get your exam back, go over it. Find out why you missed each item that you answered incorrectly. Evaluate how many questions on the exam you accurately predicted. Reflect on your successes and errors on the exam.

There are four common types of exam questions which instructors use at the college level.

1. **Short answer questions**

   These are usually (1) fill-in-the-blanks, and (2) define, identify, list, etc. Both types often require the knowledge of vocabulary, terms, laws, and facts.

2. **Essay questions**

   A. If you have a choice, choose the question(s) you will answer.

   B. Read the question carefully. Be sure you understand it.

   C. Rephrase the question as a topic sentence.

   D. Think about what you want to say. Then, briefly outline or map your answer.

   E. Write the essay, using your outline or map as a guide.

   F. If you have time, read over your essay. Make any desired changes.

3. **Multiple choice questions**

   A. First, read the question carefully. Try to think of an answer before you look at the options. When you know the answer, compare this with the options, and pick the best one.

   B. When you don't know the answer, read all of the options carefully. Eliminate the choices which are clearly wrong. Pick the best answer from the choices which are still available.

   C. Use your common sense. Even when you don't really know the right answer, you can often figure it out.

4. **Problems**

   (A) Read the problem carefully to find out what you are being asked. (B) Read through the problem again to find the information you need. (C) Organize the information in whatever way(s) helps you to solve the problem. (D) Solve the problem. (E) Check your answer with common sense and, if possible, with estimation.

Understanding how test or exam questions work is called "testwiseness," that is, being wise about the test. The more "testwise" you are, the better you'll be able to communicate effectively to your instructor through the particular questions on a test.